D1008790

WK3 Rev. 1-3
WK4 Rev chap 8
WK6 Rev ch 5, 6, 9
WK7 Rev ch 4, 7, 8

Measuring Team Performance

Steven D. Jones
Don J. Schilling

Measuring Team Performance

A Step-by-Step, Customizable Approach
for Managers, Facilitators,
and Team Leaders

JOSSEY-BASS
A Wiley Company
San Francisco

Jossey-Bass books and products are available through most bookstores. To contact Jossey-Bass directly, call (888) 378-2537, fax to (800) 605-2665, or visit our website at www.josseybass. com.
Substantial discounts on bulk quantities of Jossey-Bass books are available to corporations, professional associations, and other organizations. For details and discount information, contact the special sales department at Jossey-Bass.

Manufactured in the United States of America

Library of Congress Cataloging-in-Publication Data

Jones, Steven D.
   Measuring team performance : a step-by-step, customizable approach for managers, facilitators, and team leaders / Steven D. Jones, Don J. Schilling.
       p.   cm. — (The Jossey-Bass business & management series)
   Includes bibliographical references and index.
   ISBN 0-7879-4569-2 (acid-free)
   1. Teams in the workplace—Evaluation.   I. Schilling, Don J. II. Title.   III. Series.
   HD66.J657   2000
   658.4'036—dc21   00-009153

FIRST EDITION
HB Printing   10 9 8 7 6 5 4 3 2

The Jossey-Bass

Business & Management Series

To our families, who inspire us to make something of ourselves: Cathy, Chris, Lindsay, and Caitlin for Steve; Tamie, Scott, and Leeah for Don.

Contents

About the Authors

Steven D. Jones has worked with measuring and improving group and organization performance in applied settings for the past seventeen years. His clients have included the U.S. Air Force, AT Plastics, Duracell, Franke Contract Group, Franke Commercial Systems, General Electric, Saturn, Square D, and Sverdrup Technology. He conducts workshops on team performance measurement in the United States and Latin America. He has authored several articles and book chapters on the subject and published two edited books of case studies on work teams. Steve holds a Ph.D. in industrial and organizational psychology from the University of Houston, a master's degree in psychology from the University of Tennessee, and a bachelor's degree in psychology from the University of the South. He teaches industrial and organizational psychology at Middle Tennessee State University and is a partner in the Alignment Group. Steve has a wife (Cathy) and three children (Chris, Lindsay, and Caitlin); his hobby is climbing.

Don J. Schilling is a human resources manager for one of the world's largest and leading forest products companies. In his twelve years with the company, he has served in a variety of human resource and quality functions, focusing primarily on high-involvement strategies and statistical quality techniques.

Previously, Schilling was a senior consultant with Tarkenton Conn & Company, a consulting firm that specialized in promoting change in management practices and organizational culture. He provided training to and consulted with a broad range of manufacturing and service industries including TRW, Sarah Lee–Hanes,

Bell Canada, and United Technologies. He also held the position of quality director for Char-Broil, a market leader in outdoor cooking appliances.

Schilling's nineteen years of experience with improving organizational performance has spanned a variety of work with perpetual as well as virtual teams of both manufacturing and knowledge workers. His interest in team performance measurement stems from its pivotal role in every change effort.

Schilling received his master's degree in behavior analysis from Southern Illinois University at Carbondale and his bachelor's degree in psychology from the University of Cincinnati. He is the author or coauthor of a number of articles and book chapters on improving human performance. Don has a wife (Tamie) and two children (Scott and Leeah); he enjoys mountain biking, golf, and coaching youth sports.

Preface

Many organizations are deploying work teams on a massive scale. A recent survey by Lawler, Mohrman, and Ledford (1995) indicates that about half of the Fortune 1000 are implementing self-directed teams and that these companies plan to increase their use of teams. Since self-directed teams are the most extreme form of empowered work groups, it is clear that the use of teams of all types is even more prevalent. As work teams become empowered to make decisions and improve performance, there is an increased need for accountability. Virtually all organizations with work teams need a means for measuring their teams' performance.

This book takes the readers through a step-by-step measurement methodology that can be customized for any team. It presents a practitioner-tested approach designed for those who have the responsibility for establishing accountability systems for self-managing or supervisor-led work teams. Practical applications and descriptions of examples with different types of teams are emphasized. This book also examines the "big picture" issues that are critical to successful implementation of team-performance measurement systems. This measurement methodology has been used with hundreds of teams in dozens of organizations, and the lessons learned from these projects are incorporated in this book.

Measuring Team Performance serves many purposes. It is a resource that teams can use to develop their own performance measurement systems, and it is a training tool for facilitators to use in helping teams develop measurement systems. This book also provides a methodology for aligning team measures with

alignment with

organizational strategy, which is critical if teams are to contribute to business success. It includes an overview of larger organizational issues, so the measurement system can be understood as a systems-level intervention. This book provides an understanding of the skills necessary for supervisors, team leaders, and coaches to successfully conduct team performance feedback meetings. Finally, it includes a feedback and improvement methodology so teams can use the data from the measurement system for problem solving and performance improvement.

This book is for managers, supervisors, facilitators, leaders, and coaches of teams. It is intended for groups that design teams, trainers, human resource development practitioners, and both internal and external consultants who work with manufacturing and service teams. This book is also appropriate for students taking applied courses at colleges and universities.

Through workshops that we give, it has become clear that a book dedicated to team performance measurement is needed. While there are many books about work teams, they provide only a brief overview of team performance measurement—if the topic is addressed at all. *Measuring Team Performance* differs from other books on work teams in four ways. First, this book provides a comprehensive view of team-performance measurement, but it also goes beyond measurement to include how to use the measurement system as feedback to stimulate problem solving and track performance improvement efforts. Second, it provides extensive coverage of organization-level issues such as how to align business strategy and measurement, set goals, attach incentives to the measurement system, and reduce barriers that might hamper the success of the measurement effort. Third, this book addresses the skills needed for successful implementation of the measurement system, such as coaching, problem solving, and providing feedback. Fourth, this book is accompanied by a CD-ROM with generic examples of measurement systems that teams can customize for their own use. The topic of team-performance measurement has never been covered in this depth until now.

Structure of the Book

Chapter One offers an introduction to team-performance measurement and its basic principles: capture the team's strategy, align the team's strategy with the organization's business strategy, focus team meetings on the measurement system, use the system to stimulate problem solving, measure the few critical aspects of performance, ensure team members understand the system, involve customers in the system's development, and address the work of each team member.

Chapter Two addresses the process of developing team-performance measures. It explains how to choose dimensions of performance as well as the measures that capture those dimensions. It uses four case studies to illustrate this process.

Chapter Three examines hard-to-measure teams, including lessons learned by the authors in their efforts to measure the performance of these types of teams. Case studies of a software development team and a team of university graduate professors illustrate how these lessons can be applied.

Chapter Four describes the process of integrating the measurement system into a composite score. Three methods for constructing a composite score are discussed.

Chapter Five illustrates the benefits of team-performance measurement through the case of a Xerox team, the Hi-Rockers, which evolved from an average team to "the best of the best" at Xerox. This chapter describes the journey made by this team in making that transition.

Chapter Six illustrates the case of a team at Eastman Chemical Company. This chapter describes how this team used its team-performance measurement system to achieve strategic objectives of the organization.

Chapter Seven carries teams through the step-by-step process of computerizing their own measurement system by customizing the accompanying spreadsheet to meet their needs. This chapter also describes the process of creating feedback reports from the measurement data. The case of a Duracell chemical processing team is used to illustrate this process.

Chapter Eight examines performance improvement efforts. It addresses the skills necessary for the successful implementation of the team-performance measurement system, including coaching, problem solving, giving feedback, and conducting team meetings.

Chapter Nine describes how an incentive program can be used to keep the measurement system working over time. This chapter examines types of incentives, issues that influence the effectiveness of incentives, and methods of dividing the incentives among team members. The case of a plastics manufacturing team is used to illustrate the process of linking incentives to the measurement system. This book combines thirty-three years of experience in measuring and improving team performance in applied settings. We hope you find it helpful in creating a business partnership between your team and the company.

Acknowledgments

We would like to thank Amy Hicks Dement for conscientiously completing a multitude of details for the first author. We also acknowledge Julianna Gustafson, our editor at Jossey-Bass, whose professionalism sets a benchmark in its own right. We also wish to recognize the numerous reviewers who have made this book a better product. In addition, we thank the many organizations mentioned in this book and those not mentioned for all that we have learned from them. Finally, we want to thank the people who have attended our workshops on team performance measurement, who over the years have kept telling us, "You guys should put what you know in writing."

April 2000

Steven D. Jones
Murfreesboro, TN
Don J. Schilling
Vancouver, WA

Measuring Team Performance

Chapter One

Where to Begin

The Basics of Team Performance Measurement

Is it possible for a typical team to go from mediocre performance to the benchmark team in its organization? Within two years, Team 47 of Xerox Corporation did just that. This transformation was due, in large part, to the team's efforts in measuring and improving team performance. This team used its performance measures to become proactive in problem solving, which led to performance improvement. Team 47 is now setting performance goals higher than any team in its region—and reaching them. Team members have gone from feeling frustration and dissatisfaction to feeling pride and a deep sense of ownership in their work. Team 47 even received the prestigious X-Award, being called "the best of the best" at Xerox. (For more on Xerox's Team 47, see Chapter Five.) This team has complete ownership of its measurement system and its improvement processes. Its manager has complete confidence in the team. How can you get there with your team and where do you start?

Whenever beginning a new program such as teams an organization must ask itself, "Is this, too, just a fad?" and "How is this different from the other programs already tried?" Any program can become a fad: TQM, reengineering, process improvement, and even teams and team-performance measurement. However, the basic idea behind team-performance measurement, in this case the drive to make improvements based on group problem solving, is not a fad. Team-performance measurement provides teams with information that they can use to identify strengths and weaknesses in their performance. This information becomes the basis for problem solving concerning areas of improvement. Problem solving then leads to performance improvement through improved work processes.

Unfortunately, in many organizations team-performance measurement consists of meeting arbitrary quotas or simply counting the amount of product turned out. Many times organizations may become caught up in the administrative activity of having teams (or some other improvement effort) and forget to sufficiently connect teams to the business. The function of team-performance measurement is to connect teams to the vision and strategy of the business.

Team-performance measurement builds a platform for problem solving. It allows organizations to develop a structured process for accountability and continuous improvement. Previous research has shown that management trust is a major issue with teams. The team-performance measurement process shows management the results of team performance, so management can trust that teams are doing the right things.

Team-performance measurement is built on the same foundation as widely accepted paradigms such as Employee Involvement, World Class Manufacturing, TQM, Organizational Design, Process Reengineering, and Individual Development and Transformation. Some of the concepts and techniques of these six major schools of thought are presented in Table 1.1. One common theme among all these paradigms is increased information sharing—a main feature of team-performance measurement. Access to information eliminates the need for management layers, which results in teams's having more control over their performance improvement efforts.

Assessing Readiness for Measurement

Perhaps before even beginning to measure team performance, readiness for measurement should be assessed. Reviewing the following checklist will help to assess the extent to which managers and teams are ready for measurement.

Management Readiness

❑ Is management ready to share business information such as business strategy, costs, productivity, and customer satisfaction with the team members?

Table 1.1   Six Paradigms of Organizational Improvement

Employee Involvement	World Class Manufacturing	Total Quality Management
• Participative management • Involvement continuum • Ownership • Problem-solving skills • Team management • Group decision making • Communications skills	• Just-in-Time • Manufacturing Resource Planning • Process optimization • Synchronous manufacturing • Process reliability • Work cells • Kanban	• Prevention versus detection • Quality assurance • Statistical process control • Process capability • Cost of quality or nonconformance • Continuous improvement • Benchmarking
Organizational Design	Process Reengineering	Individual Development and Transformation
• Sociotechnical systems design • Open systems planning • Design teams • High-performance work systems • Multiskilling • Total task • Span of control	• Destroy and reinvent • Horizontal organization • Business processes • Process mapping • Process improvement teams • Streamlining • Information-process interface	• Covey's seven principles • Learning organization • Good people = good organization

❑ Have procedures been established to safeguard competitive information?

❑ Is management interested in teams' having direct contact with their customers during the process of measurement development?

❑ Is management willing for the teams to participate in determining measures and goals for their performance? Note that participation does not mean that team members will make all the decisions. All decisions will require management approval.

❑ Is management supportive of training (usually one or two hours) for all team members to fully understand the measurement system?

❑ Can key managers involve themselves in the measurement project?

❑ The project will need a champion from management; who is willing to take on this responsibility?

❑ Once the system is developed, the teams will need regular feedback (such as monthly) on their performance measures. Can resources be committed to this effort?

❑ Do managers, supervisors, and team leaders have fully developed skills in leading problem-solving sessions?

❑ Is management ready to set boundaries within which each team can make decisions? Within these boundaries, is management willing to let teams make decisions about improving their work?

Team Readiness

❑ Do team members have an interest in understanding the business and in becoming business partners, as opposed to employees?

❑ Do team members want to know how they, as a group, are doing?

❑ Are team members agreeable to having their performance displayed on a regular basis to the group and their manager?

❑ Are team members willing to be mutually accountable?

❑ Are team members interested in and able to meet with customers to discuss customer needs?

❑ Do team members have established processes and skills for solving problems in the workplace?

❑ Are team members willing to engage in solving business problems?

Eight Basic Principles of
Team-Performance Measurement

To increase the effectiveness of team-performance measurement, it is important to understand its basic principles. While it isn't necessary to follow all of these principles to the letter, it is important to note that the further an organization deviates from them, the less it will get from the measurement efforts and consequently from work teams.

1. *To capture the team's full attention, capture its strategy in the measurement system.* Team members should be involved in measurement development because the measurement system needs to model how team members think about doing their collective work. If having all of the components ready to start the assembly is the key to making the work flow more smoothly and efficiently, then measure how often all components are ready to start the job. If, based on customer input, the team thinks cleanliness is the key to meeting the customer requirements, then measure cleanliness. If you can capture the strategy at the team level through the appropriate measures, the team will want to know how well that strategy is working. This is intrinsically interesting for the team, and it tends to lead the team toward making improvements in its performance measures.

2. *Ensure that the team's strategy is aligned with the organization's business strategy.* Every business should have a vision and a strategy for achieving that vision. Some strategies are clearer than are others. Only a few organizations have business strategies that are understood by the teams, and many of the team efforts are not aligned with the organization's strategy. It takes work to attain clarity and alignment, but team-performance measurement is much easier once this is done. In fact, some teams have said that once the business strategy is understood and the team strategy is determined, the team-performance measures become readily apparent.

Today, many organizations have values by which they operate. The measurement system should also align with these values. If the values are real, they facilitate the alignment between the business strategy and the team strategy.

3. *The purpose of measuring team performance is to stimulate problem solving that leads to improved performance.* When measuring team performance, the goal is not to perfectly measure performance but to develop information that makes a difference to the team. Therefore, it is acceptable to sacrifice some precision in measurement, as long as the performance measures stimulate effective problem solving. All measurement systems for teams should be used for continuous improvement. By keeping your eye on this goal, you can avoid the following common team-performance measurement and improvement pitfalls:

- Measures that are too complex to understand
- Measures that are strictly of interest to managers
- Measures that the team cannot improve upon
- Problem-solving meetings where team members do not participate because they have no ownership of the measurement system

4. *The measurement system provides a critical focus for team meetings.* The whole reason for having teams is to improve the organization's performance. Ideally, teams will take ownership and discuss their performance measures as if they were co-owners of the business. Much of the team meeting time needs to be focused on the performance measures. At Xerox, each team member is responsible for a measure. As the meeting progresses, each member presents data from his or her measure and leads a discussion on the status of that measure's improvement efforts. In instances where problems are identified that require analysis, the team may analyze the problem on the spot or hold a separate meeting for problem solving.

5. *Measure the critical few, rather than the trivial many.* This is an age of information overload, and team members are already awash in a sea of words and data, all competing for their attention.

A measurement system should simplify the information that a team must consider by capturing the most critical aspects of the team's performance.

6. *Team members need to understand their measurement system completely.* You want people to have complete ownership and understanding of their system, to the extent that they could explain the system to someone who is not on their team. Those teams that understand their measurement system go over their feedback reports in detail during team meetings, while those that don't have that understanding skim over their reports or, even worse, just listen while the manager reads the reports to them. Either way, a team that does not completely understand its measurement system wastes valuable opportunities for improvement. The goal is active team involvement with the measurement system, which will not happen without the team members' full understanding of their measures.

7. *Involve the customers in developing the measurement system.* Customers are an essential component of the measurement process. Both external and internal customers should be involved in this process. Including customers' perspectives gets the team outside any self-serving framework that might arise when the team is deciding how it will be accountable. The idea is that any system that is closed off from energy and ideas outside itself will ultimately become less viable. By involving customers in measurement development, you get their ideas for possible measures. Asking customers what indicates when the team is doing a good job helps to strengthen relationships with customers. Just imagine what you would say to an organization which provided you with goods or services, if they asked you that question! What if they took your measurement suggestions seriously and later reported to you how they were doing on those measures? How would that sequence of events affect your relationship with that organization? Our experience is that customers want to be involved in the measurement process.

8. *The measurement system should address the work of each team member.* As the Southern expression goes, each team member

needs to "have a dog in the hunt." If any team members feel that none of their efforts are reflected in the performance measures, they will not be motivated to problem solve and make continuous improvements. This does not mean that the measurement system should capture all of each team member's efforts—just enough to keep them interested and focused on the joint goals.

Team-Performance Measurement and Team Meetings

As discussed in Principle 4, performance measurement should play a key role in team meetings. Effective performance measures stimulate team meetings that are focused on business results *and* that enhance participation of team members. Some teams do measure their performance effectively and have effective meetings. Other teams, however, have less effective measurement systems and meetings. Exhibit 1.1 describes the continuum between these effective and ineffective meetings; while there are many thematic variations in this continuum, the pattern is clear. Only when level five is reached will the organization reap the promise of teams. The continuum illustrates the point made earlier: as the basic principles of team-performance measurement are violated, effectiveness drops off rapidly.

Organizations that have ineffective performance measurement systems for their teams and have ineffective team meetings will fail to reap much of the benefit from implementing teams. Teams will lack a sense of purpose, and managers will lack confidence in the teams. In these organizations, teams will be just a fad.

Performance measurement and effective problem solving link teams to business results. It is this linkage that gives teams their purpose and gives managers a chance to develop confidence in their teams. The point being, it takes both effective performance measurement *and* effective meetings to make the equation work. One, without the other, simply is not enough. See Exhibit 1.1 to further understand this issue.

The remainder of this book will explain how to develop a system of team-performance measures so that your teams can have

Exhibit 1.1   Team-Performance Measurement and Meeting Continuum

Ineffective

1. Team has no performance measures and resists accountability. The team members focus their discussion on relatively trivial matters. The team members experience personality conflicts and a lack of reason for being a team. The team tends to blame the customer when problems arise. Organizational performance data is not open to the teams. The manager micromanages the team.

2. One team member collects data on a few measures, but the data is not presented to the team on a regular basis. When data is presented, the team speculates on errors in the data rather than solving problems. The measures tend to leave out the customer. The manager has difficulty getting full commitment from team members to solve problems and follow through on assignments.

3. One team member collects data on a few measures and presents it to the team. Team members have no buy-in to the measures and do not fully understand them, nor how they link to the business strategy. There is little or no discussion. The team focuses on isolated customer complaints. There is no team strategy.

4. Each team member is responsible for a performance measure and reports that data in the team meeting, like reading the evening news. There is little or no discussion. Excuses are made for performance that is below expectations. Team meetings drag on. There is little direct involvement with the customer. Management ends up making most of the decisions for the team. The team members complain that management won't let go of control. Management loses confidence in the team concept.

- -

Effective

5. The team has a system of measures of business results tracked over time. These measures reflect business strategy and customer needs. There is a clear team strategy. Each team member owns one or more performance measures and reports that data in the team meeting. Each team member leads a lively discussion of the causes of improving or declining performance. The team examines how it is performing in its targeted improvement areas. Team members set goals, problem solve, and agree on improvement plans for the next time period. Responsibilities are assigned to individual team members. Individuals hold each other accountable and are passionate about their piece of the business. Any team member can explain the measurement system and the problem-solving processes to a visitor. Management monitors the performance measures and fully supports the team.

6. In addition to all the activities of level 5, the team discusses ways to prevent problems in the future. Team members function as business partners rather than employees. Each team member fully understands the business strategy and there is high involvement with the customers. The team quickly brings its new members up to speed. The team is fully self-managing.

meetings like those described in levels five and six. Certainly, reaching level five entails more than just a good measurement process, but a good measurement system is central to successful team meetings.

Aligning with Business Strategy and Getting Commitment

Working with teams can become very confusing because of the inherent complexity of work in groups. If teams are empowered, won't they go off in their own directions? It is tempting to set up structures that force teams to behave in certain ways. The problem is that their buy-in is needed, or they won't do it well. In fact, the reason to have teams is to get the higher levels of performance that are fueled by participation and commitment. In addition to buy-in by the teams, two other important ingredients are needed: the teams need to focus on what the business is trying to accomplish and management needs to buy in to the team concept. The measurement process begins with team buy-in, strategic focus, and management buy-in.

Consider the following vision for a team-performance measurement system:

> An effective measurement system draws a clear line of sight between the business strategy, the customer needs, the team's strategy for accomplishing its portion of the business strategy, and a set of measures that reflects the team's strategy (See the Process Road Map in Figure 1.1). This measurement system has sufficient buy-in by the team and management so they will work together to make substantial improvements. The team uses the measurement system to actively solve important business problems, such as reducing cycle time or addressing customer requirements. As these problems are solved, the business becomes more successful.

Realizing this vision begins with establishing buy-in by both management and teams. Team-performance measurement requires a substantial effort to get this buy-in because both managers and

Figure 1.1   Process Road Map

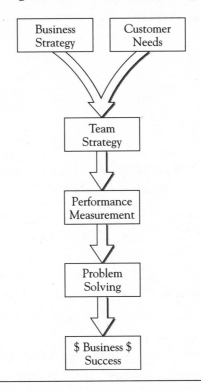

teams have issues with performance measurement. Generally speaking, traditional managers assume most of the responsibility for performance monitoring. In fact, performance monitoring has been estimated to make up at least 40 percent of a manager's job. Managers, then, are understandably reluctant to delegate much of this responsibility to a team. However, since performance monitoring has traditionally been management's responsibility, teams are reluctant to take on the responsibility of measuring and improving their own performance. Therefore, both managers and teams need to see what team-performance measurement can do for them.

Managers must be absolutely convinced that each team's measurement system is aligned with the business strategy, so that it will help the organization (and consequently, the managers) to succeed. At the team level, substantial participation by team members is needed, so they can have an opportunity to buy in to the system. Ultimately, it is the team that makes the improvements based on feedback from the measurement system regarding the team's performance. In addition, management facilitates improvement by supporting and guiding the team's efforts. Therefore, both groups need a powerful sense of ownership for the system to have a chance to succeed.

Getting Management Buy-In by Aligning with Business Strategy

When a team's measurement system captures its strategy as it aligns with the organization's strategy, management can have confidence in the measurement process. To achieve this alignment, the business strategy needs to be well articulated by management and communicated in a way that is meaningful to the team. An effectively communicated business strategy has tremendous power because it creates a channel through which the company strategy, the team strategy, and the measures of team performance can be aligned. While there are several critical factors in team implementation, alignment may be the most critical factor. Indeed, a recent market survey by the Hay Group on why teams fail found that the top three reasons concern lack of goals and lack of team accountability. Without proper alignment, slippage will occur between goals and team accountability. Why do managers sometimes withhold their full support from teams? Often it is because they believe that teams are not working in concert with the business strategy. Therefore, efforts to measure team performance (and team implementation in general) should rest on a foundation of a well-articulated business strategy.

Many companies do an excellent job of communicating their business strategy. For instance, Xerox has developed a "Vision 2000" document that explains the vision and competitive pressures out of which the business strategy for the future is forged. From this effort, teams can clearly understand why the strategy is necessary and align themselves with it. For instance, the Vision 2000 strategy encompasses transitioning to digital products and operating in an open systems environment so Xerox products can interface with other brands. This strategy then requires new products and the skills to produce and service those products.

At Wainwright Industries, a 1994 Baldridge Award winner, everyone rigorously pursues a strategy that puts people first and focuses on trust and commitment. They measure performance in the areas of customer satisfaction, product quality, financial success, safety, and employee satisfaction. In this strategy, safety and employee satisfaction drive customer satisfaction, quality, and financial success. When they have problems with their scores in customer satisfaction, quality, or financial success, their improvement plan begins with safety and employee satisfaction. Through this cause-and-effect relationship in the performance measures, a clear alignment with the people-first strategy is evident.

In this age of information overload, simplicity tends to be more compelling than complexity. Frequently, strategies are overly complex and there are too many goals. At Victoria's Secret, they understand how this obscures the line of sight and have reduced their corporate strategy from over three hundred pages to a single page. Interestingly, a recent survey on organizational complexity (Jensen, 1997) found that the second-biggest source of complexity in getting work done was due to an inability to clearly communicate goals and objectives. Effective business strategies tend to be simple, clear, and compelling visions. To the extent that leaders can articulate the strategy as a compelling vision, they can inspire teams (and individuals) to align their efforts with that vision.

Team members should be able to demonstrate an in-depth understanding of the business strategy; in other words, they need business literacy. The goal of business literacy training for teams is to make them into business partners. For managers to empower teams to develop their own measurement systems, the teams need to understand the current business realities: what things cost, critical economic choices, what the competition is doing, and the business plan for the future. As management becomes assured that teams understand the business, management will become comfortable empowering the teams.

Management needs to see the business strategy reflected in the measurement system. Management may suggest performance measures, they may adjust weighting of the measures, they may question the accuracy of the data. These are all positive signs because a good measurement system will have management's fingerprints on it.

Involving Customers in the Measurement Process

Few would disagree that understanding customer needs is inherent to an understanding of the business strategy. Yet it is not uncommon to find a disconnection between teams and their customers and especially between team measures and customer needs. Teams often use measures that are internally driven rather than customer driven. To avoid this internal focus, teams should engage in dialogues with their customers prior to and during development of team-performance measures. Both external and internal customers should be involved in the development process. External customers may be people who use the team's product or service, suppliers, and even government regulatory agencies. For example, government regulatory agencies require specific safety standards in certain industries. Therefore, it may be important for a team to measure the number of safety violations in order to meet these requirements. Internal customers are any individuals or teams within the organization that receive a team's output. For example, in an assembly plant, one of a team's internal customers would be the next team "down the line." The number of defects in the team's output may affect this internal customer's performance; therefore, the team should bring this customer into the measurement process. Some teams invite customers to the meetings where team measures are being developed. Other teams interview their major customers in individual sessions or in focus groups. Either way, these teams are bringing the customer perspective into the measurement development process. Involving customers opens up the system to new ideas and strengthens relationships with customers. It has the additional benefit of connecting the teams more closely with the customers. Southeastern Technology used to have difficulty getting teams to work weekend overtime on rush jobs. They found their teams' willingness to work rush jobs improved dramatically after the teams had interviewed customers about their needs.

Because of their external perspective, customers will have ideas for measures that teams cannot readily see. For example, while developing performance measures for a team at Duracell, the powder system team got its most important measure from its customer. The team asked the press room (its internal customer) what was most important to it. The press room team said that the consistency of the powder was most important. The more consistent the powder, the faster the presses ran. The powder system team then adopted the press room's machine speed as the most important measure of powder system quality. The point is the powder system team would never have considered this measure if it hadn't asked its customer.

Customer involvement is becoming a requirement for the best measurement systems. Teams always seem to learn something they didn't expect from customer involvement in the measurement process. We find that the best means of involving the customer is in a face-to-face meeting. We have never yet heard a company say that it wasn't worth the time and expense. In addition to allowing the team to learn something new, involving the customer dramatically raises the profile of the performance measures for both management and teams. In a recent customer meeting, the customers said they wanted their orders 100 percent correct and on time. As a result, the team members decided to support those measures in the measurement system, even though they know they do not have 100 percent control over those two measures.

In customer meetings we let the customers know we want their input as we develop the measurement system. We prepare the team members in advance with questions such as those following this paragraph. These questions are only meant as examples. Teams will certainly want to create their own. We suggest that the team stay away from self-serving questions, since the purpose is to *listen* to the customer. Sometimes we prepare the team with some listening skills practice. We want the customer leaving the meeting with the sense that "these people really listened to me."

Example Questions to Ask at a Customer Meeting

1. What do you need from this team in the short term?

2. Is one of these needs the most important? If so, which one?

3. How would you know if this team is meeting those needs?

4. How will your needs change in the next three years?

5. How can this team provide you with additional value?

It is important to make the purpose of the meeting clear to the customers, so that they don't get stuck in the mode of providing criticism. However, if a customer does become critical of the team's past performance, it goes without saying that the team should inquire into the issues and avoid getting defensive.

The follow-up to the customer meeting is critical. Customers will want to know what happened as a result of their input. We find that customers are not interested in micromanaging the measurement system; they do, however, want to see the performance measures and how the team is actively solving problems. The team's problem-solving capacity is often more important to the customers' peace of mind than any individual solution.

Getting Team Buy-In by Tying Measures to Team Strategy

Probably the greatest challenge in team-performance measurement is getting team buy-in. As mentioned earlier, teams are often reluctant to monitor their own performance. This is particularly true in organizations that have a long history of command-and-control management practices. But it is equally true in organizations such as universities that have little if any real accountability. On the one hand, it is easy to conclude that teams just don't want their performance to be measured.

On the other hand, people have a natural curiosity about how they are doing. Imagine trying to play the piano without hearing how it sounds or trying to tie a knot without seeing or feeling your fingers. People crave feedback. They want to know where they stand. The challenge is to devise a feedback system for teams that piques their interest by tapping into their inherent desire to know how they are doing.

So what do teams want to know about how they are doing? Experience suggests four questions that are of inherent interest to teams:

- How well is the business doing?
- How are we contributing to the business?
- Are our improvement efforts successful?
- How satisfied is the customer?

The common theme in these four questions is strategy. If the strategy is on target and executed well, the answer to these questions will be positive.

Do teams have a strategy? While it may not be formally stated as it is for the business unit, it exists. When you understand the team's key work processes and how those processes produce the final result, you can see the team strategy. In other words, look at cause and effect. The key to getting team buy-in is to capture the team's strategy. Capturing its strategy in the measurement system will increase the likelihood that the team will be interested in receiving feedback.

A logjam in a river creates a good model of team cause-and-effect strategy. When someone manages to loosen certain logs, all the logs start to move with the current. Moving those key logs is the strategy.

Consider a few examples. A food processing team has to produce enough products each week to meet its sales plan. The products have to meet certain quality standards, so meeting the weekly plan is the team's goal. The team's strategy concerns how it does this each week given some variability in the plan and in its own capacities. In this case, the strategy entails four key elements. First, the team must have the capacity to meet the plan. For this team, that means having the proper skill-sets among the team members, so they can efficiently run their machines and make changeovers to different products. Second, the team must follow its quality procedures, so it won't have waste that causes the team to have to make more product just to make the plan. In this team's business, quality is highly affected by good housekeeping practices, so this is also a key element in the team's strategy. In addition, the team finds that if it can run a little ahead of schedule during the first part of the week, it can handle changes in orders and machine malfunctions that occur during the week.

Certainly, more could be added to the strategy, such as preventive maintenance, safety, and cooperation between shifts, but the point is to capture the thinking of the team as simply as possible. If these other elements are critical in the team's thinking, they should be added. If not, leave them out. In other words, reduce the trivial many to the vital few and capture the essentials in ways the team thinks about its work.

Teams think about their work in strategic ways. You can discover how a team thinks about its work by asking questions that get at what causes their work to go well. It's useful to ask questions such as these:

- What has to happen for your work to flow smoothly or to reduce your backlog of work?
- What are the key ingredients to making your project successful?

- What one change, if it were made today, would result in your team's wasting less time?
- What do you have to do to delight the customer, and what do you have to do so that is possible?
- What one thing, if it were done poorly, would have the most negative impact on your work as a team?

These questions will help reveal the team's thinking and strategy. Where disagreements arise among team members, a leader or facilitator may have to help the team articulate and resolve its different strategic views. This resolution will further solidify the strategy.

What signs are there that the strategy is correct? Look for some degree of passion. If the team gets excited talking about it, that's a good sign. If, after listening, the team can summarize it, and the members say, "Yes, that's it," that confirms it. If someone suggests taking away an element of the strategy and the team puts up a fight, there's buy-in to the strategy. Often, each strategy has one key, and that key will elicit the most passion from the team. Once the strategy is correctly understood, it can be graphed with a cause-and-effect diagram, such as that in Figure 1.2.

**Figure 1.2   Cause-and-Effect Diagram of Food Processing
Team Strategy**

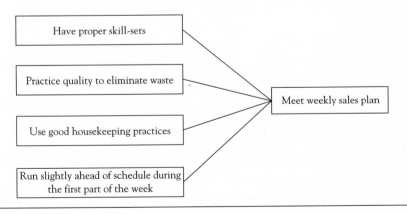

Once the team strategy is understood, it needs to be aligned with the business strategy. Alignment helps to get management buy-in. In this case, the business strategy is consistent with the team strategy: always meet the sales plan, while keeping costs down and producing a consistent product. Once you make sure the team strategy and business strategy are aligned, you can develop measures that capture the team strategy. That will get the team to buy in.

Different teams within the same company may have different strategies. This is a good thing, as long as the strategies align with the business strategy, because it is the key to getting buy-in. Just as businesses differentiate themselves with strategy, teams tend to do the same. They take pride in figuring out their strategy. Think of it as their "secret recipe." Capture the strategy in measures and they will want to see how that strategy plays out.

To illustrate how team strategies differ, consider another example. Through group discussions, an assembly team at Square D Company might determine that reducing defects would reduce cycle time, improve productivity by reducing overtime, and improve on-time delivery to the customer. The team might also understand that a key to achieving its goals was the timing with which it received all the parts, materials, and engineering drawings needed to assemble the product. If everything was ready for the members to start a job on time, then their cycle times were reduced. In addition, delivery times were met and productivity was high. Their strategy is shown in the cause-and-effect diagram in Figure 1.3.

Team-performance measurement requires a participative approach for two reasons. First, team members must take ownership of their measures to maximize their performance on those measures. A good test of ownership is to see if the team would defend those measures against the threat of losing them. This happened with the Square D assembly team's measure of percentage of jobs for which all materials were ready on time. As a test, we suggested that they drop this measure. They put up a fight. We knew that measure had captured their strategy. Second, the purpose of having

Figure 1.3   Cause-and-Effect Diagram of Assembly Team Strategy

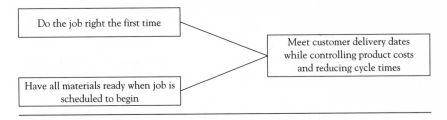

the measurement system is for the teams to problem solve, and problem solving requires participation. Therefore, teams should participate in the development of their measurement systems. Expect differences between measurement systems for different teams—this is a part of participation. However, the teams do not need to make all the decisions about their measures to establish ownership. If the teams make some of the decisions, that is enough for them to buy in to their system. In most organizations, teams do not expect to freely determine all their own measures. They understand that they must make decisions within certain boundaries. Typically, these boundaries are determined by management or a steering committee made up of managers, support staff, and team members.

Role of the Steering Committee

A steering committee typically serves as a representative body during team implementation. The steering committee provides initial guidance in team measurement and provides an integrating function throughout the measurement process. The steering committee may develop a list of suggested or required measures for teams with similar functions. These measures may reflect corporate or plant business strategies. For instance, the steering committee may suggest—or require—that all manufacturing teams have measures of productivity, quality, cycle time, and on-time delivery to the customer. Around these four measures, teams could have some latitude to modify the measures and add one or more of their own, thus reflecting their team strategy.

During the time that the teams are developing their measurement systems, the steering committee reviews the team strategies and measurement systems. This check ensures that the teams are working on the right things. In measurement systems that set performance standards and distinguish measures in terms of their relative importance, the steering committee reviews these team decisions to ensure alignment with the larger organization. Another purpose of a review by the steering committee is to ensure that teams have measurement systems that are equally challenging.

When Team Cooperation Is Crucial—Sharing Measures Across Teams

Teams have a natural tendency to focus on work over which they have control. Team measurement systems, especially if rewards are attached, strengthen this tendency. In their efforts to improve their piece of the business, teams often become less inclined to help other teams. Yet many organizations need cooperation between teams to succeed. In fact, most major successes in organizations probably occur across team boundaries.

If team A gets ahead of its work schedule, should it put effort into things that will help itself, such as cross-training and preventive maintenance, or should it help team B if it is behind schedule? If helping team B is crucial to the business strategy, say by reducing overtime and maintaining delivery deadlines to the customer, build a measurement system that encourages cooperation. If the business strategy does not depend on team cooperation, the teams can develop completely independent measurement systems.

Early in the measurement process, the steering committee or some other body should address team cooperation. Key questions to ask concern the strategic importance of interteam cooperation, whether it is ongoing or occasional and what measures could be shared across teams. The greater the importance of cooperation across teams, the more measures the teams should share. Where low to moderate cooperation is required, teams can share one or two measures such as productivity or customer satisfaction. In the extreme case, where organizational success is completely dependent on team cooperation, team performance would be measured at the business unit level. Thus, teams would share all the same measures. Alternatively, as with the powder system team described earlier, each team could adopt at least one performance measure based on results from a downstream process so as to have an indicator of how well it was promoting the overall business.

Summary

The goal for the first phase of measurement development is to get buy-in by management and team members. Buy-in is achieved gradually, not all at once. Keys to achieving buy-in are clarifying the business strategy, involving the customers, capturing the team strategy, and using participation. In addition, it is critical to align the business strategy, customer needs, and team strategy. At the end of this phase, teams should clearly understand the business strategy and the customer needs. Also, teams should have a clear understanding of their own team strategy. As a quality control check, each of these points of understanding should have some energy around it.

To the extent that cooperation across teams is crucial to business success, the teams may have to share performance measures. A steering committee may determine which measures a team should share.

Assessing Your Team

Note: "Assessing Your Team" is included at the end of most of the chapters in this book. These activities allow you to work through the information in each chapter. They are steps in the measurement process that allow you and your team to work through the process to develop your own measurement system. You will need the information generated in many of these sections to take advantage of the material on the CD-ROM packaged with the book, as described in Chapter Seven.

1. List two or three of your organization's key values.

2. Describe your organization's vision.

3. What is the business strategy for accomplishing the vision?

4. Identify and describe your team's customers (both internal and external).

5. List the products or services that each of your team's customers need. Circle the most important needs.

6. What are your team's goals?

7. Describe your team's strategy as it supports the company's business strategy (how will it accomplish those goals, what will it emphasize, what will cause other things to happen, and so on.)

Chapter Two

Developing Team Performance Measures

Measuring What Matters

Two employees are talking:

Martha: It seems like we are just wasting time in team meetings.
David: I hear you, we rarely talk about anything important. We have some performance measures from corporate, but no one on the team understands them and I don't see how what we do has any effect on them. We need to forget about teams and team meetings and get back to doing our jobs.

Purpose of Measurement

Teams need the correct measures or they will waste their valuable time and lose confidence in the team approach. To select the correct measures, it's important to maintain focus on the purpose of measuring team performance. As discussed in Chapter One (Principle 2 and Principle 3), the purpose is to stimulate continuous improvement on measures that align with the organization's business strategy. While the measures should be accurate, the purpose is *not* perfect measurement. It is better to have an acceptable measure that a team will work to improve than a perfect measure that the team does not understand or accept. When a team works to improve a measure, its members collect systematic data, solve important business problems, develop action plans, and follow through on their plans.

Family of Measures

Since "what gets measured gets done," it is important to measure all of the important areas of a team's performance. If an important area is left out, it will tend to get less attention. This problem becomes magnified if pay is tied to performance. The family-of-measures approach allows for a group of measures that cover the entire domain of the team's performance. If the team can answer yes to the following four questions, its family of measures is properly comprehensive.

1. If we do well on all these measures, will we be a high-performing team?

2. If we do well on these measures, will we meet or exceed customers' expectations?

3. If we do well on these measures, will we help the company succeed in its business strategy?

4. If we do well on all these measures, will we succeed at our own team strategy?

Dimensions of Team Performance

In the beginning, it is tempting for the team to simply begin identifying measures of performance. However, this gets the team into the details too soon, and the team will lose sight of the big picture. A series of steps should be followed in the development of team performance measures, as illustrated in Exhibit 2.1. As recommended in the Chapter One, the team should begin by understanding business strategy, customer needs, and team strategy (the first three steps in Exhibit 2.1). As these three issues come into focus, the team can identify the areas in which it needs to perform well (dimensions of performance). Sometimes these dimensions are called "key results areas" or "products," but they are the major areas within which the team has to do well to be a high-performing team as determined by its own strategy. Understanding the business strategy, the customer needs, and the team strategy is the secret to identifying the right dimensions of team performance. The dimensions provide a map of the areas in which the team will identify performance measures. Example dimensions include product quality, customer satisfaction, training, productivity, responsiveness, innovation, and safety.

Exhibit 2.1   Process for Developing Team Measures

Step	Activity
1.	With managers: What is the organization's business strategy? Make sure that the strategy is clear to the teams. Review the organization's mission or vision statement.
2.	With customers: What do they need, both short term and long term? Determine what the customer needs in terms of results that will help the customer's business:

- Quantity? (volume, rate)
- Quality? (accuracy, usefulness, reliability)
- Cost? (efficiency, budget)
- Timeliness?

Do the customers have a single most important need?

3.	With teams: What is the team strategy?
4.	With teams or steering committee: What constitutes success? Identify three to seven dimensions of performance.
5.	With teams or steering committee: How can we measure success?

- Brainstorm potential measures.
- Review available measures in current organizational records.
- Create new measures if necessary.

| 6. | Select five to ten best (that is, the critical few) measures of team performance. |

- Test against criteria for good measures.

Repeat this step until all measures meet criteria.

| 7. | With management: Are the measures acceptable? |

- Expect management to make adjustments.

| 8. | With team: Do the measures really work? |

- Test measures with real data.
- Make modifications based on experience.
- Develop feedback reports and format for presentation (explained in Chapter Seven).

Choosing the Optimal Dimensions

On the one hand, if the team selects too many dimensions, administration of the measurement system will become a burden. On the other hand, if key dimensions are omitted, important opportunities for improvement may be missed. The goal is to select a few precise dimensions that capture both the team and business strategy. The secret to choosing the appropriate dimensions lies in understanding cause and effect at the team level. Typically, there will be one or two key causes and three or four key effects. Three to seven dimensions are optimal for most teams. Teams that have difficulty determining the optimal dimensions probably need to spend more time clarifying their business and team strategies. The following case study illustrates how to choose optimal dimensions.

Case Study: Photocopier Service Team

A team from a Fortune 500 company that services photocopiers and office machines (not Xerox) developed a performance measurement system. The business strategy was clear: generate revenue and comply with the laws governing inspection of postal meters. Customer feedback indicated a need for quick response and reliable repairs. This led the team to identify the following three dimensions:

- Customer Service
- Revenue
- Required Activities (for legal compliance)

In this example, it should be clear how the business strategy and customers' needs lead directly to the dimensions of team performance. In Table 2.1, an examination of the measures for each of these dimensions further reveals the business strategy, the customer needs, and the team strategy. The measurement system is aligned with customer needs via the first four measures and the business strategy via the last three. In addition, the fifth measure reflects the team's strategy: have parts available for repairs.

Table 2.1   Dimensions and Measures for a Photocopier Service Team

Dimension	Measure
1. Customer service	1. Average response time to respond to a customer call
	2. Response time targets met (percent of calls answered within prescribed limits)
	3. Call backs (percent of repaired equipment operating beyond prescribed service intervals)
	4. Mean time to repair (percent of service calls completed within the prescribed repair time for the equipment being serviced)
	5. Calls incomplete due to parts (percent of service calls that could not be completed due to lack of available parts)
2. Revenues	6. Billed labor (dollar amount of labor performed other than for existing maintenance agreements)
	7. Dollar value of maintenance agreements sold or renewed
3. Required activities	8. Percent of target met each month for postal meter inspections, as required by law

Measures of Team Performance

After establishing the dimensions of team performance, measures can be identified for each dimension. Usually one measure per dimension is sufficient, but some dimensions occasionally require more. As a rule, four to ten measures are optimal for most teams. Service teams tend to have more measures than manufacturing teams. Large cross-functional teams tend to have more measures than small teams whose members perform similar tasks. Temporary teams need the fewest measures.

Table 2.2 presents a set of quality control checks for good performance measures. This is just a suggestion; each organization should develop its own quality control checks.

Table 2.2   Quality Control Check for Performance Measures

Category	Issue	Example
Strategy	Is the team's strategy evident in the measurement system and is it aligned with the organization's business strategy?	If providing high-quality products is part of the organization's business strategy and, subsequently, the team's strategy, the measurement system should include measures such as number of defects per unit.
Customer perspective	Do one or more measures reflect the customers' view of the team's performance? How will the customers react to this set of measures?	Customers require that products be shipped on time, so the team may use delivery time as a measure.
Results-based	Does this measure represent a team accomplishment, or the critical cause of a result?	When the work is done right the first time, the amount of scrap will be small.
Team-oriented	Does the measure represent a result accomplished by the team as opposed to an individual?	If only one member of the team is responsible for equipment maintenance, the rest of the team may resent being evaluated according to the amount of machine downtime.
Influenceable (Control)	Can the team have a significant influence on the measure?	If the team has no possible influence on deliveries, it cannot be held accountable for on-time shipping. Caution: most teams can find a way to influence key measures by changing their processes.

Table 2.2 (Continued)

Category	Issue	Example
Corruption resistant	Is the measure resistant to tampering and falsification?	Would a team accurately report its own or some other team's number of quality defects?
Accessible	Does the data required by the measure already exist or is it easy to get?	While an organization may not currently track cycle time (number of days each unit takes to assemble), that data is relatively easy to collect.
Frequent feedback	Can performance on the measure be reported frequently (usually at least monthly)? Quarterly data may be frequent enough for customer surveys.	A team wants to use a customer survey, but it is only available on a yearly basis. Can the company administer and report the surveys quarterly or monthly?
Line of sight	Can each team member draw a line of sight between what they do and several of the measures?	Several team members receive new material on a daily basis, so if there is no measure of receiving, one should probably be created.
Understandable	Can each team member fully understand the measures?	Complex productivity ratios are difficult to understand; less complex ones, such as the ratio of dollar value produced to labor hours are easier to understand.
Linkage to other teams	Is there a measure or two that the team can share with other teams to foster teamwork across team boundaries?	Customer satisfaction, accounts receivable, and productivity can often be shared across teams.

Developing Measures

Most of the team's measures already exist somewhere in the organization. The problem becomes finding them and separating the critical few from the trivial many (Principle 5). Developing dimensions before identifying measures helps teams sort out the key measures. This procedure allows the teams to establish their focus before examining the often bewildering array of potential measures.

As discussed in Chapter One, many organizations use a steering committee to sort through the available measures. This saves time for the work teams and helps ensure linkage to the organization's business strategy. This procedure works particularly well in organizations where there are many teams doing similar work. The steering committee can develop a list of suggested or required measures for the teams. Teams can take some or all of their measures from this list.

Most high-performance teams, however, will want to develop at least one measure of their own. Doing so gives them ownership and a deeper understanding of the measurement process. The measure or measures that they develop themselves will probably reflect their team strategy. Teams are typically passionate about what they create for themselves. As noted in Chapter One, if someone tries to take one of these measures away and the team fights to keep it, that's ownership. It may sound funny to talk about passion with regard to performance measurement, but the truth is that if there is no passion somewhere in the measurement and feedback system (which includes the problem-solving process), great improvements won't happen.

Case Study: Xerox Service Team

At Xerox, the teams that service copiers and high-speed printers all have a common set of performance measures determined at the corporate level. Their measurement system is described fully in the Xerox case study in Chapter Five, but some aspects are relevant here. The Hi-Rockers team—already a winner of the X-Award for performance management—wanted to replace one of the corporate-developed measures with one of its own measures for response time. All Xerox service teams used to respond to a service request with respect to a response time generated by a standard formula, which covered a variety of possible situations. The teams were measured by their actual response time compared to the formula time. Most teams thought it was too risky to let the customer determine the response time, not the Hi-Rockers. The team members reasoned that if they provided the best service in the business, the customer would not request unreasonable response times. Although they were advised not to, they implemented the customer-driven response time. This new measure fit their team strategy: stay ahead of the problems. If a customer says that a certain machine needs to be fixed by tomorrow at 10 A.M., the Hi-Rockers try to get it fixed by 4 P.M. today. Their repairs are completed early over half the time. They also spend about 50 percent of their time preventing problems, so their customers never experience problem with their machines. Even with a tougher response time measure, the Hi-Rockers are still the highest-performing team in Xerox. Xerox has since adopted the customer-driven response time measure across the company.

Case Study: Assembly Team

Square D Company has a number of teams that assemble large circuit breakers. Each unit is approximately the size of a closet. Each assembly team has four dimensions and four corresponding measures determined for them by a steering committee. These four dimensions and measures are as follows:

- Quality (the number of defects per unit)
- Productivity (catalog value in dollars of the units assembled divided by the number of work-hours to assemble each unit)
- Cycle Time (the number of days each unit takes to assemble)
- On-time Shipments (the percentage of units that are shipped to the customer on time)

Many of the assembly teams just accepted these four measures from the steering committee. However, some assembly teams added a fifth measure of their own that reflected their strategy. One assembly team added a dimension called "Assembly Start," which reflected the percent of jobs where the necessary materials—the engineering drawings, the raw materials, and the semi-finished components—were available when each job was scheduled to begin. This dimension and its measure reflected the team's strategy. If a job was missing some materials, this slowed down the assembly process. Because of the size of the circuit breakers, they clogged the production line if the assembly could not proceed quickly. Then the cycle time was slower, productivity dropped, and customers might not get their orders filled on time. The team strategy aligned well with the business strategy, which was to respond quickly to the customer order at the lowest cost. Quality was also an important part of the strategy, because it is cheaper and faster to assemble an order right the first time than it is to trace down the problem in hundreds of possible wiring connections.

Management Oversight

As a team is developing performance measures, management will want to review these measures for completeness and alignment with business strategy. Management needs to maintain a dialogue with the teams during measurement development. Depending on the stage of development of the teams, management may initiate ideas for measures, or may expect teams to develop measures for review. Either way, it should be clear that management's involvement is critical to the process. In fact, if we find management making adjustments to the teams' performance measures, that's a good sign. It means that management is buying in to the measurement system.

Common Problems

A number of problems often occur when teams develop their own measures. First, there is the problem of choosing measures and goals that are easy to improve but are not key to the team and business strategy. For instance, in an organization that is faced with a need to reduce costs, a team may not readily see how it can help reduce costs, so it chooses measures of reports completed and training delivered. These measures are easy to do well on, but they have little to do with reducing costs. This often occurs in organizations that change to a team culture from a strict command-and-control culture, where the teams lack a true sense of empowerment and partnership in the business. Benchmarking with similar teams in other organizations may help the team to choose more challenging measures.

A second common problem occurs when teams avoid identifying measures over which they do not have complete control. This is one of the biggest issues in team measurement. The true criterion here is influence, not control. For example, a team may not want to measure its parts inventory because it feels it has no control over the parts system. Yet if getting parts is critical to the team's success and the team can at least influence the system, perhaps it should measure parts. Another team may not want to measure delivery time to the customer because its members do not drive the trucks. Perhaps the team can work with management to influence the trucking company through a data reporting arrangement. Bringing the customer into the process often helps resolve this issue. Some of the greatest improvements in team performance have come about as a result of a team's improving a measure over which it originally thought it had no control.

A third problem concerns teams' tendencies to focus internally and avoid thinking of measures that promote cooperation with other teams. Experience shows that this third problem seems to grow out of a team's desire to develop its own identity. While this tendency is generally positive, it can lead to some measurement problems for the organization. Many opportunities for improvement in organizations require cooperation across teams. Therefore, teams may need one or two measures that capture efforts to cooperate across team boundaries. As mentioned earlier, measures such as customer satisfaction and plantwide productivity require cooperation across teams. Without guidance, teams may not see these "big picture" opportunities, since their tendency will be to focus internally.

Management should be alert to these three common measurement problems and any others specific to the organization. No one else except management can exert the proper influence on the teams to prevent or resolve these problems. Experience indicates that prevention of these problems is much more effective than solving them once they are fully developed.

Worry about the problems that may occur with a high-involvement process leads to an extreme position: management identifies all the measures for the teams. This approach results in a different problem—lack of ownership by the teams. If teams do not develop ownership of their measures, they will not make the kind of improvements expected of high-performance teams. The lack of ownership by teams often leads to a cycle where management provides data on performance measures to teams, the teams do not look for ways to use the data to make substantial improvements, most team meeting time becomes wasted, and then both management and teams get disillusioned with their efforts. There is tremendous waste in this scenario: waste of precious meeting time, waste of opportunities to make improvements, and waste of efforts to connect teams with business results. This pattern is difficult to reverse, and if left unchecked it is likely to undermine the team concept.

Management can prevent this lack-of-ownership problem by setting up a system that empowers teams to make measurement-system decisions when the teams are ready to make them. Teams do not have to make all measurement decisions to develop ownership. Typically, people do not expect to make all the decisions about their measurement system unless they have been working in a self-directed team for a long time. As long as they can make some of the decisions about the measures, the relative importance of the measures, how to solve problems in team meetings, or how incentives will be distributed, they can develop ownership.

Testing Period

Once the team and management have approved the team's measures, the measurement system needs to be tested with real data. The initial set of measures can be best thought of as a prototype that will need some modification after testing. When a team develops new measures that have not been used before, these measures are at the idea stage. The measures may sound good, but the team will not know the validity and practicality of the measures until they have been tested with live data. This testing period usually lasts three to four months. The goal is to find possible problems with the measures and make modifications even as the team begins improvement activities. Once the measures are modified, the team can put its improvement efforts into high gear.

Case Study: Storage and Delivery Team

A storage and delivery team wanted to measure how well it resolved discrepancies between items received and items it had ordered. Sometimes items would be received by the team that were slightly different from what it had ordered. These were called discrepant items, of which there was a running list. The team's initial idea was to measure this as the number of discrepancies cleared off the list divided by the total number of discrepant items. When tested with real data, this measure actually got worse over time as the team solved problems and removed discrepant items from the list. The team cleared the easiest items first; this decreased the total number of discrepant items, leaving the more difficult items. As a result, the ratio (number of items cleared to number of discrepant items) actually got smaller (worse) over time. This measure indicated that the team's performance was getting worse as it cleared more and more items off the list. This was because there remained only a few difficult items left to be cleared. After testing the measure, the team changed the measure to number of discrepant items left to be cleared. The new measure worked well, and they used it for several years.

A team evaluates measures with data to see if the measures perform as expected. As a result of this testing, the team can make adjustments to the measures. Sometimes these adjustments entail a change in the calculation, like that of the storage and delivery team. Other times, testing may reveal that a measure has to be redefined. The Square D assembly team, discussed earlier, identified a measure of on-time delivery to the customer. After testing with actual delivery data, the team found that the assembled product could sit for a long time in the shipping department due to last-minute changes in delivery dates by the customer. As a result, the assembly team redefined its measure as on-time delivery to the shipping department. The on-time date to the shipping department was determined by taking one day off the promised delivery date to the customer.

Case Study: Plastics Manufacturing Team

The AT Plastics manufacturing team runs a state-of-the-art plastics extrusion operation in Peachtree City, Georgia. Their ultra-clean facility makes a product with very low levels of impurities, as required by their customers. Their business strategy is to increase market share by making a strong impression on potential customers and maintaining that relationship with a high-quality product and service. This impression hinges on the ultra-clean manufacturing process and state-of-the-art equipment, and on the capabilities of the team to prevent and solve problems. The plant encourages customer visits. Since the team is self-directed, team interactions with customers are a critical part of the marketing strategy. Team members give plant tours and answer customers' questions.

The team members must be very knowledgeable about their processes, energetic, and able to answer tough questions to make the initial positive impression. After the sale, they must maintain the relationship with the customers by consistently delivering a high-quality product on schedule. In order to make a profit, the team has to control costs. Because the plant is highly automated, there may only be four team members running the plant at any one time.

This team understood that to achieve a good relationship with the customers, team members would have to be very satisfied with their jobs. Only if their morale was high could they convey a sense of excitement about their work to the customers. They also knew they needed to communicate well among themselves, with the sales department, and with their suppliers. In addition, they needed to have a high-quality product, control costs, meet production schedules and prevent accidents. All team members answered yes to the question, "If you do well in all of these areas, will your business be successful?" Figure 2.1 charts these dimensions of team strategy.

Initially, employee satisfaction was not included in the system. After some discussion, the team members decided that the business could not be successful unless employees were satisfied with their jobs. Recall that the business strategy positions the team members as part of the marketing effort. Therefore, the team strategy requires the employees to be excited about their work, so they can communicate that excitement to the customer.

Figure 2.1 Team Performance Dimensions

Following these discussions, the team developed its performance measures. Top management reviewed these measures to ensure they aligned with the corporate business strategy and values. Several changes were made as a result of this review before management agreed to the family of measures shown in Table 2.3. One of the changes involved aligning the measurement system with the corporate values. Some questions in the employee survey were written to address corporate values (for example, respect, working together, continuous learning, and recognition). Some of the questions in the communication survey addressed other corporate values (such as openness and taking responsibility). The remaining corporate values were covered by measures in the system (safety, quality, providing added value to customers).

In addition to approving the measurement system, top management agreed to base variable pay on team performance. This

Table 2.3   Dimensions and Measures for a Plastics
Manufacturing Team

Dimension	Measure
1. Employee satisfaction	1. Employee Survey: average score
2. Communication	2. Communication Survey: average score
3. Product Quality	3. Cleanliness Test: number of particles
	4. Additives Test: percent pass
4. Cost Control	5. Budgeted/Actual: expenditures of fixed plus selected variable costs
5. Production	6. Percent Prime Product
6. Safety	7. Number of Lost Time Accidents
	8. Number of Approved New Safety Procedures
7. Customer Relations	9. Customer Satisfaction Rating: overall score (a customer developed index that contains items for on-time delivery, quality, accuracy of packaging labels, and accuracy of invoices)

Source: AT Plastics, Inc. Used by permission.

decision meant that the measurement system would require a single composite score that summarized all ten measures. (This procedure will be explained in Chapter Four.) After receiving management approval, the team tested each of the measures with actual data gathered over a three-month period. The testing revealed that minor changes were required for the cost control measure so it would be easier to collect and to understand.

Summary

The goal is to design a measurement system that the team will use to make improvements, not to design a set of perfect measures. By following the process steps given in Exhibit 2.1 and the guidelines given in this chapter, a team can develop a good set of performance measures. These steps provide a basic structure for the measurement process. Each organization should modify them to fit its own situation. For instance, some companies begin the process with training on business literacy. Other companies introduce benchmarking into the process in the beginning. We strongly suggest that all companies involve the customer in the measurement process and also that all teams develop the background knowledge they need to fully understand the business strategy. Finally, buy-in by both the team members and management is essential.

Assessing Your Team

1. Using your responses to items one through seven at the end of Chapter One as a context, identify the dimensions within which your team has to do well to be maximally effective. Pay particular attention to the team strategy. The dimensions should reflect the team strategy as it supports the business strategy.

2. List your dimensions in the grid in Table 2.4 and identify one or more measures for each dimension. Keep the total number of measures to no more than ten. Fewer is better.

Table 2.4 Dimensions and Measures

Name of Team:

Dimension	Measure
1.	
2.	
3.	
4.	
5.	
6.	
7.	

Chapter Three

Hard-to-Measure Teams

Quantifying Performance

Two members of a knowledge team are talking:

> *Sarah:* You can't measure what we do. We just try to exceed the
> customer's expectations.
>
> *Chris:* Yeah, I know, we already measure so many things in this
> company. But those are the easy things to measure, not the
> most important things we do.

The performance of some teams is more challenging to measure
than that of others. The performance of teams with clearly defined
outputs is obviously easier to measure than that of teams with no
tangible end product. On the one hand, most manufacturing teams
and service teams with repetitive functions (such as processing
insurance claims) present little difficulty in developing measures.
Indeed, the most difficult task with these teams may be to reduce the
volume of possible measures to the vital few. On the other hand,
research and development, marketing, multifunction accounting,
university faculty, engineering, human resources, and other support
teams present a measurement challenge of the highest order.

In some sense, the hard-to-measure challenge has become synonymous with the nearly two-decade-old white-collar productivity
initiative. Starting in the early 1980s, there was a lot of talk about
whether organizations could measure and subsequently improve the
performance of white-collar and knowledge workers. In the past two
decades, methods for measuring hard-to-measure teams have
emerged. And they are still evolving. This chapter will examine why

we should bother to develop measures for white-collar, knowledge-work teams, presenting lessons we have learned and several practical methods for those who would like to accept the challenge. The insights and suggestions outlined in this book are derived from the authors' experience with several companies, the findings of the American Productivity Center's two-year research project on white-collar measurement (1986), and the groundbreaking work of the Tarkenton Conn & Company consulting firm. The second author was a senior consultant at Tarkenton Conn & Company from 1981 to 1986. Many of the concepts and methods developed by this firm with respect to white-collar measurement can be found in Boyett and Conn (1988a and 1988b).

Why Measure Knowledge-Work Teams

So the performance of white-collar and knowledge-work teams is an extremely difficult thing to measure. Many managers and change agents have given up on their vision of scorecards for support teams, sometimes even within organizations with exceptional performance measurement and feedback systems for core-work groups (Schilling, 1998). With such formidable odds, why try?

Knowledge work is on the rise. The new workplace has witnessed a dramatic shift from jobs that produce products to jobs that produce information and knowledge. The employment cost of managers and professionals is staggering. Knowledge work has become the biggest piece of the productivity or performance pie. Although the topic is difficult to quantify, our experience suggests that knowledge and information waste exceeds more traditional product waste. Business and industry can't afford not to increase the performance of knowledge teams—and measurement, of course, is the first step.

There is also a very human side to the white-collar-work story. With no measures of output or contribution, management often intuitively feels that a reduction of force in a support function is OK or even justified. They may even believe that it might motivate the remaining employees. With no end to the downsizing threat yet in sight, workers can not afford not to measure their team's performance. Measuring the "hard stuff" is clearly worth our effort and resources.

Lessons Learned from Hard-to-Measure Teams

In addition to discovering it takes a lot of work, we have learned several other lessons from our experience with hard-to-measure teams.

1.   *White-collar and knowledge-work teams resist measurement.*

Most white-collar workers have no history of measuring their performance and some view it as a practice with application only to lower-paid production or service employees. Many also believe you can't measure creativity or judgment, major ingredients of knowledge work. Although the vast majority of knowledge-work teams are in the business of providing a service or intangible product rather than creativity or judgment, the associated resistance is often difficult to penetrate. It is as if measurement somehow takes the magic out of the work and renders it less valuable. In addition, there is a pervasive belief that the team has nothing to count. It is difficult to convince team members that delivery of services or information can be quantified.

2.   *The precision of the measures pales in comparison to the use of the measures.*

Frequently armed with high levels of education, analytical skills, and creativity, knowledge-work teams can seem intent on identifying the "perfect" measures. But performance measurement for these teams more closely resembles parenting than any exact science. If parents waited to take action until they could make perfect decisions, would they ever decide? Endless deliberation, the proverbial "paralysis through analysis," would test the patience of the entire family. In most cases, being as good a parent as you know how to be is good enough, as long as your actions are consistent. The measurement for hard-to-measure teams is much the same.

Decent measures that are reviewed and used consistently are much better than no measures or perfect measures that are not used for performance improvement activities. Moreover, we have found that as the team uses the measures, modifications are easily made. Most of the time they just need to get started.

3. *Measures for the sake of measurement are useless.*

Organizations that take their improvement vows and set forth a prescription for all teams to have performance measures create a great deal of pressure to comply. But as we have discussed, the output of knowledge-work teams is at best difficult to quantify. Counting the number of pages an administrative assistant word processes in a week or the number of lines a programmer generates per day may be valid performance measures. But how meaningful are they? To what extent can they be used to feed improvement efforts? Hard-to-measure teams not only require assistance with their measurement development, they also need realistic expectations regarding time to complete the task. Otherwise, measures for measurement's sake will likely appear.

4. *Hard-to-measure teams see themselves as overhead, rather than as business partners.*

The true mission and objectives of support teams are often vague and disconnected from the organization's strategy and the team's customers. Therefore, the basic principles for team measurement become even more critical, especially the principles concerning strategy (Principles 1 and 2) and the customer (Principle 7) that were covered in Chapter Two. The "Total Measurement Development" method described later in this chapter guides teams through a strategic and customer value assessment, plus an accountability and data analysis, to ensure the team understands its role in meeting business and customer requirements.

5. *These teams require the highest level of involvement in the measurement process.*

This book has emphasized a participative approach in which all teams are involved in determining their measures. But externally developed measures are particularly fatal for hard-to-measure teams. First, the high level of resistance can begin to be broken down by involving team members in the design and development of measures. Second, only the team members can clarify the team's often ambiguous purpose and agree on the outputs and desired results that serve as a basis for developing measures. Even though the process should be assisted by a skilled facilitator well versed in measurement technology, there is no substitute for involving those who do the work in how to measure the work.

6. *Hard-to-measure teams must expand the types of measures included in their measurement system.*

Results measures, which are emphasized throughout this book, can fail knowledge-work or support teams in several ways. One, a significant portion of the team's output may not be reflected by a results measure because the measure is a function of the work of multiple teams. The team is but one link in a chain of teams that support a process that crosses team boundaries. Support teams are much more likely to be involved in such horizontal processes than are core-work teams, who are typically focused on primary products or services. Two, results measures can obscure the most significant performance problems, especially in continuous processes.

Hard-to-measure teams must consider process- and job-level measures to supplement—but not replace—results measures. As described in more detail later in this chapter, process-oriented measures can be used to quantify the outputs of a process contained within the team's boundaries as well as the outcome of a process step or activity. They can also be used to measure dimensions of the team or high-involvement system (for example, number of improvement ideas generated). Job-oriented measures quantify the outcome of behaviors and activities performed by individuals. If a substantial proportion of team members or individual performers have the same job (that is, produce the same outcomes), the job-level measures may be accumulated in some fashion into a team measure.

7. *Some hard-to-measure teams are not really teams.*

Really not teams?

Organizations often form groups of knowledge workers that actually don't meet many of the criteria for being a team. They don't share a common purpose. The team boundaries don't enhance the detection, correction, or prevention of critical variances. And the members don't depend on one another to accomplish common results. Indeed, we field numerous questions about team performance measurements from our clients and conference participants for which the answer is, "you don't really have a team." Often, the so-called team is just a collection of individuals doing separate jobs with little collaboration. In this instance, much of the team's performance may be measured through individual performance appraisals, supplemented by a few team-level measures. The Zigon Performance Group (www.zigonperf.com) has developed a useful methodology for these situations.

It is interesting to note that the ability to identify team performance measures is one way to test team membership and boundaries. If a group of individuals are not a team, it will be tough to get them to behave like one. But assuming you have a true team and you understand the measurement principles described thus far, you are ready to apply one or more of the measurement development methods that follow to your hard-to-measure teams.

Methods

The literature is replete with discussions concerning the difficulty of measuring the performance of white-collar and knowledge-work teams. It seems no obstacle has been overlooked. In contrast, our posture is both optimistic and constructive. Rather than simply talk about the difficulties, which we have acknowledged, our intent is to talk about what hard-to-measure teams can do to quantify their performance. First, we will present the broad range of measure types available, which is particularly helpful to hard-to-measure teams (see Lesson 6 earlier in this chapter). Then we will review several methods for identifying or developing a team's performance measures. Although we do not present any new or startling principles about measurement development, in our experience, the methods possess the utility and simplicity to get the job done. So if you tried to measure knowledge-work teams before and gave up, here is your chance to give it another try.

There are several types of measures available to teams, as displayed in Figure 3.1. Measuring team results, not activities, is the preferred practice for many reasons already explained in this book, but the main point bears repeating. Results are valuable—they pay the bills and provide the capital for growth. Activities cost and should be minimized. You need only the vital activities required to produce results that meet business and customer requirements and, ultimately, establish competitive advantage. However, we have also pointed out that hard-to-measure teams must expand the types of measures included in their scorekeeping.

Understanding Figure 3.1 and the five types of measures shown is a prerequisite for proceeding to the methods for developing measures.

Organization Results Measures are the quantified product of multiple cross-functional processes (order fulfillment, product development, and so on) and are the culmination of team and department results. The measures of organization results can be classified in three major categories:

- Operating results: Tons of good product produced, recordable incident rate (safety), on-time delivery percentage, and so on.

- Customer satisfaction: Documented perceptions of product or service from external customers, returned goods as a percentage of amount of product shipped or in dollars of customer credit, and so on.

- Financial results: Net sales, operating earnings, return on net assets, and so on.

Team Results Measures are the combined, quantified effect of the steps and activities performed within the team boundaries that are part of a larger, cross-functional process (process step and

Figure 3.1 Types of Measures

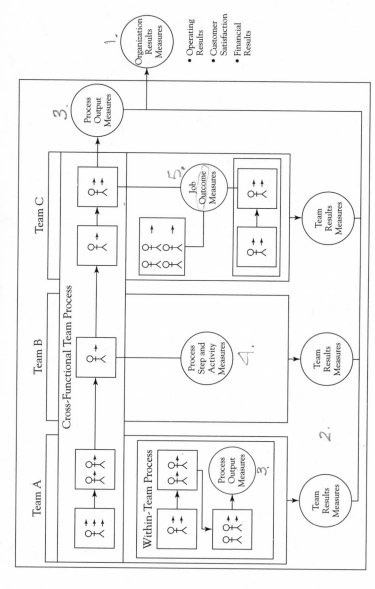

Source: The inspiration for this graphic came from Rummler and Brache, 1995, p. 136.

activity measures, such as percent of orders entered on time by the internal sales and customer service team as part of total order fulfillment process). They also reflect the outputs of processes totally performed within team boundaries (within-team process output measures, such as number of payroll errors made by accounting team) and the outcomes of behaviors or activities performed by one or more individuals (job outcome measures, such as percentage of engineering change orders per drawing issued for a product engineering team). These measures are often referred to as measures of the team's products or services.

Process Output Measures are the quantified end product of cross-functional or team processes performed across team or departmental boundaries—sometimes difficult to distinguish from organizational results when looking at core processes such as manufacturing—and within-team processes that are completely performed within the boundaries of the team. The latter are often considered synonymous with, or at least a major part of, the team's primary products and services.

Process Step and Activity Measures are the quantified end product of one or more steps or activities that are part of either a cross-functional or within-team process, such as percentage of on-time journal entries as part of a monthly financial closing process. These types of measures may not be the most meaningful team measures for the long term but are often necessary short-term tools to effectively fix or manage a process.

Job Outcome Measures are the quantified end product of behaviors or activities performed by individuals as part of steps or larger activities in within-team or cross-team processes, such as response time to customer phone calls by retail clerks (customer relations process). They also include actions or tasks not easily recognized as part of a single process but performed often enough by one or more individuals to be considered a primary "function" of the team (that is, part of a class of behaviors or tasks common to several processes, such as percentage of on-time reports to management for a financial analysis team). Note that "job outcome" could have been named "job output." The term *outcome* is used to help teams more easily distinguish between process outputs and the end products of individual behavior.

Familiarity with the various types of measures can in itself facilitate the development of measures for hard-to-measure teams. In our experience, a thoughtful scan of Figure 3.1, accompanied by brief definitions and examples of the measure types, has spawned insights quickly translated into measures. However, a more systematic approach is usually required. The following six measurement development methods are presented roughly in ascending order of the effort and resources they require.

Method 1: Chaining

Behavior analysts have long known that most tasks or activities are composed of several behaviors linked together in a sequence, or chain. Typically, one starts with the first response in the chain, proceeds to the next, and so on until the ultimate or last behavior in the chain is performed. For example, learning to drive a car solo can involve a chain of behavior including attending a driver's education class, taking driving lessons from a reputable training agency, driving with a parent, and so on until the novice is on the road alone. But why not start later in the chain, provided the risks are reasonable? Such an approach can be used with measurement development, and there is only one link to make in the chain.

Measures are best developed by the simple chain shown in Figure 3.2. Some readers may recognize the strong influence of Thomas Gilbert here (see Gilbert, 1978, p. 124). The heart of the chaining method is the answer to the question, What evidence already exists that the team has performed in some fashion? Since you cannot observe any form of accomplishment (be it result, process output, or even the outcome of job behavior) while it is happening, you need some evidence that the accomplishment

Figure 3.2 Measurement Development Chain

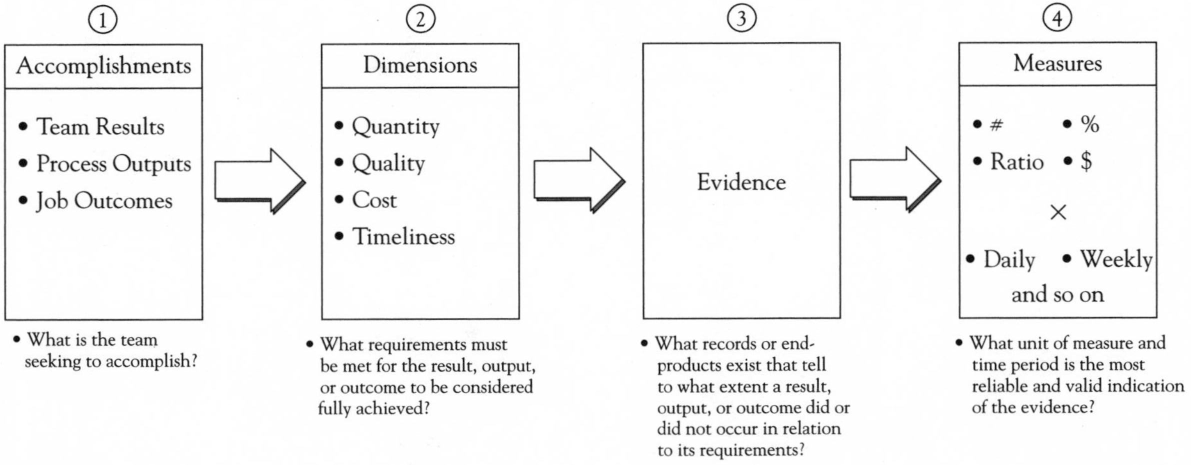

① Accomplishments

- Team Results
- Process Outputs
- Job Outcomes

• What is the team seeking to accomplish?

② Dimensions

- Quantity
- Quality
- Cost
- Timeliness

• What requirements must be met for the result, output, or outcome to be considered fully achieved?

③ Evidence

• What records or end-products exist that tell to what extent a result, output, or outcome did or did not occur in relation to its requirements?

④ Measures

- #
- Ratio
- %
- $

×

- Daily
- Weekly and so on

• What unit of measure and time period is the most reliable and valid indication of the evidence?

has or has not occurred. If you identify the records and end products that are collected on the team's performance, you need not go back any earlier in the measurement development chain. A helpful way to identify this evidence is to ask, When all the team members have gone home, what records and other tangible products of their performance can be found?

The evidence will often surprise you. For example, there are typically completed forms, reports, correspondence, phone logs, and a host of electronic documentation that testifies to the work performed. Categorize this evidence and the conversion to actual measures is somewhat obvious (for example, percentage of back-logged expense reports processed).

A word of caution, however, about this temptingly quick and dirty method—existing evidence of team performance may not represent the team's primary products and services. Naturally measures developed by this method must be checked against the criteria described in Chapter Two before they are included in the performance measurement system. But it is an easy way to start.

Method 2: Menu Selection

Not interested in cooking up measures from scratch? Then you may just want to select a few from a menu of possible measures. Our second method for developing measures for hard-to-measure teams involves three steps that reflect three of the four links in the measurement development chain (see Figure 3.2).

1. Identify the primary products and services of the team (Link 1—the team's desired accomplishments).

2. Define expectations for each product and service (Link 2—the requirements or dimensions of each output).

3. Select the measures that are most appropriate for a given product or service from a list of measures employed by teams with similar outputs (Link 4—units of measure).

In brief, to use this method, you begin by answering a few questions about the team's outputs and then select the measures you wish from the Appendix at the back of this book—a menu of measures compiled from the authors' experience and other sources.

Step 1: Identify the team's primary products and services. Hard-to-measure teams are often baffled or overwhelmed by the task of identifying their products and services. They are either confused by the notion that the terms *product* and *service* can be applied to their unique work or paralyzed by the prospect of specifying all the things they do for so many people. To get started, we have found it helpful to first identify the team's internal and external customers.

Begin by clarifying that it is usually sufficient to identify the team's key customers—those 20 percent of the customers who receive 80 percent of the team's output. It is also helpful to note that key customers typically include the end users of the team's products and services. For example, for a risk management department conducting monthly inspections of the fire suppression sprinkler system, the regulatory body (local fire department or fire marshal) and insurance underwriter are the customers who are the last to receive the inspection report. Other customers who receive the report prior to the end users might be the facility manager and maintenance department. Although the expectations of the intermediate customers are important, the requirements of the end users carry the most weight. In our experience, most hard-to-measure support teams should limit their customer list to three to five major recipients of the team's work.

The team then identifies the specific products or services supplied to each of the identified customers. It is important that these products and services be defined as discrete, tangible outputs. Think about it from the perspective that team members transform inputs into observable products and services that would not exist if not for the work or processes performed by the team. Quite simply the team is answering, What does this customer receive from our team? We have found it useful to define outputs in a simple noun-verb structure stated in the past tense—for example, "performance scorecards developed."

Step 2: Define expectations for each product and service. There is a range of activities a team can engage in to identify customer expectations for a given product or service. One activity is to construct and deliver a questionnaire to select individuals in the customer organization, asking them to specify the most important characteristics of a product or service, how you are currently performing to those expectations, and what your team might do differently to better fulfill their requirements. Such an in-depth customer analysis is better matched to more comprehensive approaches such as Method 6—Total Measurement Development—described later in this chapter. In the menu selection method, it is enough to put yourself in the customer's shoes and identify the critical requirements for each product or service supplied. A set of four requirements have seen widespread use: quantity, quality, cost, and timeliness. (The use of these "critical dimensions" also appears to have originated with the work of Thomas F. Gilbert—see Gilbert, 1978, pp. 45–47.) For each requirement there are subdimensions or questions that facilitate the team's view of the customer's expectations.

CRITICAL DIMENSIONS

Quantity

- Volume: Does the product or service need to be provided in certain amounts?
- Rate: Does the product or service need to be provided in certain amounts in a specified time?

Quality

- Accuracy: Does the product or service need to be provided without errors (commission or omission)?

- Usefulness: Does the product or service need to meet certain standards to be judged good enough to use?

Cost

- Efficiency and Budget: Does the product or service need to be provided using not-to-exceed levels of resources (labor, materials, overhead)?

Timeliness

- Delivery: Does the product or service need to be provided by a specified time?

Step 3: Select measures from a menu of measures. The team is now ready to match measures from a list like that shown in the Appendix to the products and service requirements identified in the first two steps of this method. Of course, the measures selected should meet the criteria of good measures explained in Chapter Two. There are also a few additional criteria to keep in mind in selecting measures from a menu—rules that help avoid making premature choices.

First, collection of the data necessary to calculate the measure must be realistic. The value or benefit of having the measure should outweigh the cost or effort of obtaining it. The team needs to ask if it would be any worse off without the measure. The team must also ask, Can the measure be combined with another measure to provide more information with less effort? Second, the measure must be sensitive to changes in how the team performs its work. If people did things differently, would the measure reflect the changes? Third, it must be possible to report progress on the measure at least monthly. And last, the measure should minimize outside influence or contamination. That is, How likely are events external to the team to influence the number regardless of how team members perform? If the menu does not contain measures that meet these criteria and match the team's outputs, we suggest one or more of the other methods in this chapter.

Method 3: Benchmarking

Benchmarking can be used in several ways, as described later in Chapter Eight. With respect to measure development, it involves identifying teams similar to your own that are truly exemplary performers—and then identifying how they measure their performance. The team must first specify its primary outputs (see Step 1 in Method 2) to ensure it finds a comparable group. Then the search can begin. There are several sources from which a team might identify high-performing teams with similar products and services.

The best place to start is within your own organization. Many companies have standardized processes for sharing best practices. In these cases, it would take little effort to learn how the teams that exhibit such practices measure their performance. Professional associations, particularly those associated with quality improvement (such as the American Productivity and Quality Center), are also good sources of information. Similarly, professional or trade publications frequently report success stories. Although the article may not explicitly address performance measurement, there is usually a lead contact to get your inquiry started. Indeed, if your contacts go smoothly there may be little involved beyond asking what measures they use, how the data is collected, and how the indicators are calculated.

But benchmarking does not always go smoothly. You may have difficulty finding a high-performing team comparable to your own. After searching, the team might conclude that no one else does the same work as they do. In our experience, these cases are often the result of the preoccupation with precision discussed in Lesson 2 earlier in this chapter. While another team may not employ the same processes or perform the same job functions as your team, there are frequently very common products and services. For example, many hard-to-measure support teams create documents. The measure of this product could be much the same across different types of documents provided the requirements were similar (for example, accuracy, timely delivery).

A team may locate an exemplary team with similar outputs only to find it won't divulge any information. Naturally, your competition may not wish to share practices or corresponding performance measures they perceive as giving them an advantage. The most obvious way to circumvent this obstacle is to look for the best outside your industry. This is especially applicable to support teams that provide essentially the same products or services regardless of their organization's business line.

In summary, if you are resourceful, one of the easiest methods to develop good measures is to identify how the best do it. However, if your team has tried all three methods described thus far with little or no success, there are yet more options.

Method 4: Functional Analysis

We have frequently encountered hard-to-measure teams who stubbornly maintain that they produce nothing. They have no outputs that can be seen and certainly none that can be measured after the team members have gone home. Educational activities and structured exercises fail to convince them that their processes and functions result in some product or service. So if you can't beat them, join them.

Although it is arguably a matter of semantics in some cases, we sometimes elect to dispense with the concept of results (or outputs or outcomes) in favor of job functions within the team. Rarely have we found team members who would not list what they do in great detail, often producing several pages of daily tasks and duties. When these responsibilities are sorted into five to ten categories, the outputs of these clusters of activities are usually evident. For example, in a cost accounting department it usually turns out that several team members make different types of journal entries during month-end closing. Although these entries are conspicuously different, require different expertise to perform, and occur at different points in the process, in the end, they may all be stated as an output—journal entries completed.

But a functional analysis is more than a clever way to elude resistance or get to results by a different means. Experience with and research on white-collar measurement reveals that there is a wide variety of work performed by knowledge workers. One key to measuring this work is to recognize the different types and the measurement schemes that seem to best fit each. White-collar knowledge work falls into five categories (Boyett & Conn, 1988a).

Type 1: The Factory. Some knowledge work is much like work performed by manufacturing or production teams. That is, many white-collar teams have very tangible and quantifiable outputs. This includes processing functions in which some type of repetitive task is performed on a document (matching to another document, checking for accuracy, and so on) and then an output is created to confirm that the task has been completed (for example, data entered electronically, log book entry completed). This type of knowledge work is relatively easy to measure in the same fashion as its counterpart factory work. Measures of quantity (such as claims processed per hour), quality (such as ratio of errors to units processed), cost (such as cost per unit processed), and timeliness (such as percent of batches processed on time) are all applicable.

Type 2: Support Functions. Many knowledge or white-collar workers perform all or parts of processes that support core production or service processes. Maintenance, production and personnel scheduling, and training are examples of this type of work. It is often best measured based on the impact it has on the core process it supports. For example, a measure of the maintenance team is percent uptime on the equipment maintained. Although such support functions may not have complete control of the result because of its link to a core process, the team usually has significant influence on the performance measure. If in fact they do, the team members will eventually consider it to be a meaningful measure of their own performance.

Type 3: Recurring Projects. Many hard-to-measure teams primarily perform project work. One type of project work involves projects that follow a standard process with a relatively predictable cycle time. In other words, certain steps are completed within a scheduled time frame. Most accounting and report preparation functions are examples of recurring project work—billing, payroll processing, quarterly sales reports. Because it is repetitive and time sensitive, good measures of this type of work focus on quality (rework, complaints), cost (actual versus planned), and timeliness (elapsed time versus standard time).

Type 4: Quick Response Projects. In contrast to recurring projects, quick response projects typically do not follow a standard process—they are "special"—and must be completed rather quickly. Knowledge workers such as engineers or financial analysts, who must respond to impromptu requests from internal or external customers, perform this type of work. These workers must often produce special reports or responses in a few hours or a few days. As with recurring projects, measures of quick response projects involve quality, cost, and timeliness. But here, time-oriented variables receive special emphasis with measures such as elapsed time to planned time, on-time rate, and response time (time from request to start of work).

Type 5: Long-Term Projects. The last type of knowledge work involves functions such as long-range marketing, product development, or research of various forms. Such work typically extends over months or years before a distinguishable output materializes (for example, new product introduced). Long-term projects usually have a budget and a well-documented project plan or timeline. As a result, meaningful measures focus on compliance with the budgeted cost and project schedule. How many times have you heard long-term project teams proudly proclaim, "We came in ahead of schedule and below budget." Intermediate measures center on the timely completion of critical steps in the project plan and errors

errors

that may affect schedule compliance (for example, rework or steps that must be redone).

Many hard-to-measure teams will get bogged down as they attempt to apply the strategy-results-dimensions-measures cycle underlying the measurement development strategy set forth in this book. Those guiding the team must be flexible and willing to listen to team members enumerate their responsibilities in non-result style. By categorizing these responsibilities, meaningful measures will come to light.

Method 5: Process Measurement

Earlier in this chapter we recommended that some hard-to-measure teams expand the types of measures included in their measurement system. Measures of team results are not enough for many knowledge-work teams, not because they simply need more indicators for the team's scorecard, but because these teams are likely to be involved in key processes that cross team boundaries. Measures of the critical subprocesses or activities that affect the overall process performance are crucial to maintaining and improving these horizontal processes. As Geary Rummler and Alan Brache write in their widely read book, *Improving Performance: How to Manage the White Space on the Organization Chart* (1995, p. 166), "If we had to select the single action that would make the greatest contribution to lasting Process Management, it would be the development and installation of a process-based measurement system." In Chapter Eight, we examine the skills, steps, and tools of process management. But as always, process improvement and management begin with process measures.

The first step in identifying process measures is to identify those subprocesses or activities within the team's boundaries that are most closely linked to the team's primary products and services (that is, the desired team results). This is the work fundamental to the team's capability to meet customer and business requirements. You can't measure every subprocess or step or the team would collapse under the weight of excessive measurement, so only the critical processes and activities within the team should be measured.

When identifying critical team processes or process steps, the team must understand the customer and business expectations for each of their primary products and services (see Method 2—Menu Selection—earlier in this chapter for how these expectations are determined). The team brainstorms all the processes that contribute to the achievement of these expectations—the work that adds value to the customer and advances the business. The processes or process steps to be measured are naturally those adding the most value and having the highest potential for improvement. For example, a team of human resource professionals may perform in total or in part well over a dozen processes such as compensation planning, employee relations, and management development. However, only one or two of the processes might contribute to the team results that help the organization realize its current strategy. Perhaps one or two more are not as critical but must be addressed because of internal customer complaints (for example, if benefit administration is fraught with errors it needs to be fixed even though it would have a low priority if it were running smoothly).

At the team level, we have found that process measures fall into four categories—within-team process output, process step output, process effectiveness, and culture change. The first two are standard types, monitoring continuing activities found in almost all organizations, while the others are special types that occur as needed.

The first standard type, *process output measures*, quantifies the end product or output of a process performed within the boundaries of the team. These outputs and corresponding measures are often viewed as the primary products or services of the team and, hence, are not usually distinguished from measures of the team's results. Returning to the human resource example, this team may be completely responsible for the employee selection process. In this case, the percent of position vacancies filled within ten days of posting is an end-of-process measure, but it is also likely to be a primary service provided by the team and therefore perceived to be a team result rather than a process output measure, particularly if all or most of the team members are involved in the service.

The second standard type, *process step or activity measures*, quantifies the outputs of one or more steps (subprocesses) that are part of either cross-team or within-team processes. Continuing with the human resource team example, the team may be responsible for several of the initial activities in the performance appraisal system including development of an assessment form, training those delivering feedback, and matching performance levels to specific compensation increases. In an organization of novice managers or coaches, the training on how to assess performance and provide feedback may be critical to the overall business strategy. Therefore, it would be beneficial for the team to track performance in relation to this training with measures of subprocess effectiveness (for example, "quality" ratings of trained managers' appraisals by those appraised) or measures of subprocess efficiency (for example, cost per manager trained), or both.

Flowcharting the team's processes and subprocesses will help identify the steps or activities that are worthy of measurement (see Chapter Eight for more about flowcharts). Look for places where the output of a step or activity undergoes a state change. That is, look for points in the process where the team has added value to the output of the previous step. State changes occur most frequently when an output changes hands from one team member to another or when the work changes form (for example, hard copy information supplied by another team is reorganized and entered into a computer).

The first of two types of special process measures tracks *processes or subprocesses needing substantial improvement*. In Chapter 8, Performance Improvement Methods, we discuss how to identify "broken" processes and reengineer them the way they should be. In order to establish reengineered processes and ensure they do not revert to their original form, specialized measures are required, at least temporarily (see Step 5 of the Reengineering Model in Chapter Eight). For example, a team within the finance department may experience difficulty processing customer credit applications in a timely fashion. Once the process has been redesigned or streamlined, it might track the percentage of late credit applications until acceptable performance stabilizes.

The second special type of process measure involves quantifying dimensions of the high-involvement process or other efforts aimed at what is often referred to as *culture change*. As we discuss in Chapter Eight (the Assess phase of the PDAI improvement cycle), these measures are typically used to track the progress of the entire organization. For example, the percent of teams that have developed performance measures can be a telling indicator of a company's improvement initiative. However, similar types of measures can be put to good use at the team level, especially in the early stages of team development. For instance, teams routinely develop team meeting checklists to help establish the effective and efficient use of meeting time. Such checklists can easily be translated into an ongoing measure of team meeting performance (percent of checklist items performed satisfactorily, percent of time spent on problem solving, team member ratings of participation level, and so on).

Process measures provide an alternative to results-based measures for hard-to-measure teams. Granted, quantifying the products and services of many teams can be difficult. Process and subprocess outputs are often more evident to such teams. Processes requiring improvement offer another, albeit temporary, source of measurement. And teams at all levels of maturity may find it helpful to measure progress toward their high-involvement vision.

Method 6: Total Measurement Development

The last method for developing team performance measures combines elements from several methods described in this chapter into a total, holistic process. It is based largely on a process developed by the Tarkenton Productivity Group, an international consulting firm, who successfully applied the method to a number of hard-to-measure teams throughout the eighties and early nineties. It has since been enhanced several times and continues to generate creative measures for both blue-collar and knowledge-work teams unable to otherwise quantify their performance. The method is a highly structured and participative process that works best with teams of eight to ten under the guidance of a trained facilitator. If the total team size is greater, we suggest the selection of representatives for a measurement subteam. The process generally involves a weekly session of two to four hours for each of the method's ten steps, resulting in a total elapsed time of two to three months. This allows time between sessions to gather and summarize information needed to complete each step. Of course, the length of the sessions and time required for the whole process will vary with the number of team members and the degree of difficulty in collecting data. The facilitator should be skilled in group leadership as well as measurement principles and concepts such as those described in this book.

Exhibit 3.1 provides an overview of the method. After the team receives some basic education about performance measurement the members focus on identifying the team's desired results (primary products and services) from four perspectives: the strategic self-view, the customer view, the accountability view, and the information system view. Consensus regarding key team results is reached. The results are then converted to measures through a series of steps starting with identifying the business and customer requirements for each result and culminating in the selection of five to ten measures for the team's scorecard.

There is nothing magical about the methodology. It is quite simply a series of questions about what a team seeks to accomplish. The team organizes and agrees on the critical accomplishments (key team results or primary products and services) and the best indicators that the requirements for each of these accomplishments have been achieved. High involvement of all participants is the essential ingredient. The total measurement development method

Step	Activity
	Exhibit 3.1 Overview of Total Measurement Development Method
1.	Provide basic education in performance measurement.
2.	Identify what the team wants to accomplish that improves the total organization's competitive position.
	(Strategic Self-View)
3.	Identify what the team's customers would like the team to accomplish.
	(Customer View)
4.	Identify what management holds the team accountable for accomplishing.
	(Accountability View)
5.	Identify what accomplishments are considered important based on the information that the team currently collects and reviews.
	(Information Systems View)
6.	Consolidate and agree on key accomplishments.
7.	Determine business and customer requirements for each key accomplishment.
8.	Identify evidence of performance for each requirement.
9.	Brainstorm potential indicators.
10.	Select five to ten measures for the team's scorecard.

is appropriate for hard-to-measure teams willing and able to commit the high level of resources and participation required.

Step 1: Provide basic education in performance measurement.
There is no need to develop team members into measurement experts. They need only enough motivation and knowledge to effectively and efficiently complete the process steps. There are four general topic areas that should be addressed.

1. *Basic team and communication skills:* Active listening, assertiveness, conflict resolution, and group decision making should be covered, with an emphasis on the latter. We have

found that the basic principles of consensus as well as one or two voting and ranking techniques are sufficient for good group decision making, provided fundamental communication skills are prompted and reinforced by a skillful facilitator.

2. *The role of measurement in improving performance:* The dual function of measurement with respect to confirming and reinforcing behaviors as well as redirecting and correcting behaviors that lead to desired results should be emphasized. In addition, the following benefits should be discussed:

A   Promotes a common team purpose

B   Aligns team activities with organization strategy

C   Communicates performance expectations

D   Reveals improvement opportunities and signals need for problem solving

E   Affords feedback against expectations and tracks progress

F   Serves as a basis for reward and recognition

3. *Fundamental units of measurement:* The five most common types of measurement units should be explained:

Frequency counts—the number of times an event occurs.

Ratios—the number of times an event occurs divided by the number of times the event could have occurred.

Percentages—the number of times an event occurs divided by the number of times it could or should have occurred out of one hundred opportunities.

Dollars—the monetary impact of an event occurring or failing to occur.

Judgment scores—points or ratings based on a predetermined scale or set of standards or criteria.

4. *The need for evidence or permanent record:* Since the method drives the identification of desired accomplishments or results rather than activities, by definition, team

members must understand that measures require some evidence that an accomplishment has or has not occurred.

Step 2: Strategic Self-View. The first vantage point for identifying the team's key results is the team's own perspective in relation to the needs of the business. The process is similar to strategic planning. It starts with collecting and analyzing sources of direction external to the team. This includes corporate and other higher-level goals, objectives, and strategies. Second, the team should examine values, vision, and mission statements developed by the team. Within this context, the team is then ready to answer six sets of questions that disclose the team accomplishments that will make the most significant contribution to the organization.

1. What are the accomplishments unique to this team (that is, the results or outcomes that only it can achieve)?
2. Looking out into the future three to five years, what would this team have accomplished for the company that would give it the greatest sense of satisfaction?
3. What advantages does this team have compared to similar groups within or outside the company? What accomplishments must the team achieve to maintain these advantages over the competition?
4. What disadvantages or weaknesses does this team have compared to similar groups within or outside the company? What accomplishments must the team achieve to overcome these weaknesses in relation to the competition?
5. What things outside of this team's control affect its ability to perform well? What accomplishments must the team achieve to minimize the negative effects of these things outside its control?
6. What changes in the business and company environment are likely to have an impact on the team? What accomplishments are important to achieve for the team to adapt to these changes?

Remember, the team must express all its responses as discrete, tangible accomplishments or outputs. See Step 1 of Method 2—Menu Selection earlier in this chapter for a brief explanation of how to define outputs in a simple noun-verb structure. Two case studies, one involving a software development team and the other a university graduate program, are presented later in this chapter to illustrate alignment among business strategy, team strategy, and team performance measures.

Step 3: Customer View. The second perspective for identifying the team's primary results identifies what each of the team's key customers need, want, and value. The team begins by identifying all the internal and external customers who receive the team's product or service. As part of this step, the team can survey actual customers. However, we have found that most teams can reliably assess their customers' expectations by performing the following activities:

1. List the team's primary products and services. (See Step 1 of Method 2—Menu Selection earlier in this chapter for help.)

2. List the customers who are the major recipients of each product or service.

3. For each customer of a particular product or service, complete the sentence, "The customer will be satisfied if—"

4. Identify common expectations across products or services and customers and ensure these expectations are expressed in terms of outputs or accomplishments.

Step 4: Accountability View. Accountability is one of the most frequently uttered words in organizations of all shapes and sizes. Clearly, the assignment of accountability is crucial to performance management. But sometimes it is difficult to establish working accountability—a sense of responsibility and ownership for a particular result. Often there is confusion concerning where such responsibility lies. In this step, the team members clarify those accomplishments for which they are accountable by putting themselves in the shoes of the manager within whose scope of responsibility the team falls as well as those of the next higher level manager.

The manager's view and that of the upper manager (in parenthesis) are assessed with the following questions:

1. What are the major objectives the team would have to accomplish over the next year to earn an "excellent" rating from the boss (the boss's boss)

2. If the team could accomplish only one of the major objectives, which would the boss (the boss's boss) most want to see?

3. What objectives or work does the boss (the boss's boss) review regarding the team on a regular basis?

4. What does the boss (the boss's boss) consider to be the team's major successes during the past year?

5. What does the boss (the boss's boss) consider the team's major opportunities or challenges in the coming year?

6. What are the critical costs that the boss (the boss's boss) expects the team to monitor and control?

Naturally, the team, or a member thereof, could interview the managers to obtain their direct response rather than infer how they believe the managers would respond from the managers' past patterns of behavior. Regardless of the approach, after the questions have been answered, the team analyzes the responses for consistencies and inconsistencies in expectations. As always, the team must also ensure the expectations are expressed as outputs or results.

Step 5: Information Systems View. The last of the four perspectives regarding the team's critical accomplishments requires the team to collect and examine all available sources of performance information that are currently either produced or received by the team. This includes all forms, logs, and other documents used in whole or in part to track performance-related data. Organizations and the teams within them have a strong tendency to monitor work that is important regardless of what other performance they say is important. Therefore, it is crucial in identifying key results to study existing documentation and measurement practices. In addition, a careful review of existing performance records facilitates the discovery of potential data sources for new, more meaningful measures.

For each document:

1. Circle or otherwise highlight the vital few numbers that the team or managers look at.

2. Define the purpose and uses.

3. Identify the source of the data.

4. Specify the necessary calculations.

Here are a couple of questions that are helpful in identifying the vital few numbers:

- What are the key performance records or numbers managers expect the team to monitor, control, and be familiar with?

- What performance data do managers review with or ask the team about on a regular basis?

After reviewing and agreeing on the key numbers, their purpose, sources, and calculations, the team should record this information for use in the next step.

Step 6: Consolidate and agree on key accomplishments or results. In earlier steps the team has identified key results it regards as important to the organization's competitive position (Strategic Self-View), outputs the customers say are important (Customer View), accomplishments management says is important (Accountability View), and information considered important by virtue of its current tracking. In this step, the team must identify recurring themes and patterns among the key accomplishments (Steps 2–4) and cross-reference them with existing data (Step 5). Working with a composite list of accomplishments, outputs, or results, the team reaches consensus on five to ten critical results that should serve as the basis for developing performance measures.

To help consolidate the list of key accomplishments the team should first answer a few simple questions:

- Where is there duplication?
- What outputs or results can be combined if reworded without losing the intent?
- How can the results be grouped to reflect recurring themes or patterns?

As the team nears the five-to-ten target for key results through voting and ranking, further consolidation can be achieved by cross-referencing the vital few numbers that were identified in Step 5. Simply list these numbers or records next to the key results to which they are related. Some numbers may not relate to the increasingly smaller set of results. If so the team should decide if additional results should be formulated to match off with this performance information.

Step 7: Determine requirements for each key accomplishment or result. The team should now have five to ten key results. All results have certain requirements that must be met if the result is to be considered truly achieved. As previously discussed, the most common dimensions or requirements are quantity, quality, cost, and timeliness. The means to determine which requirements apply to each key result was presented earlier in this chapter (refer to Step 2 of Method 2—Menu Selection for information on defining expectations for each product or service).

Step 8: Identify evidence of performance. The team must determine what observable and countable events or records provide evidence of how well the requirements (quantity, quality, cost,

timeliness) of each key result have been met. In Method 1—
Chaining, earlier in this chapter, we noted a helpful way to identify evidence of performance is to answer the question, "When all
the team members have gone home, what records or other tangible
products of their performance can be found?"

Step 9: Brainstorm potential indicators. Armed with knowledge
of the most common types of measures (frequency counts, ratios,
percents, dollars, judgment scores) and perhaps some sample measures from the Appendix, the team can begin to match measures to
the results-requirements-evidence schema.

Step 10: Select five to ten measures for the team's scorecard. The
team again uses consensus decision making to make its choices
of team performance measures. In our experience, one of the most
effective decision-making processes at this point is to evaluate each
potential measure against these criteria for good measures:

- *Team oriented:* Does the measure represent a result accomplished by the team as opposed to an individual or a few team
  members?

- *Global:* Does the measure reflect an overall goal of the team as
  opposed to a subgoal? (Note: With only five to ten measures
  available, teams usually can't justify measuring subgoals.)

- *Control:* Can the team have a significant influence on the
  measure?

- *Corruption resistant:* Is the measure resistant to tampering and
  falsification?

- *Accessible:* Does the data required by the measure already
  exist or is it easily obtained?

- *Frequent feedback:* Can performance on the measure be
  reported at least monthly?

- *Measurement family:* Do the measures collectively span the
  scope of the team's responsibility?

- *Customer perspective:* Do one or more measures reflect the customer's requirements for the team's performance?

The Total Measurement Development Method is the most comprehensive process for developing performance measures for hard-to-measure teams. Conceptually, however, it is quite simple. The process essentially consists of two major thrusts: consensus regarding key team results and development of corresponding measures. The systematic picking and poking at the team's performance ensures the team understands what it needs to accomplish and why before it decides how to actually measure it. The ten steps require considerable investment of team resources and commitment. It isn't for everyone and we have provided five other methods requiring considerably less effort. All these methods, of course, can be employed by any team. However, we have found the methodological structure mainly necessary only with hard-to-measure teams— teams like the ones described in the following case studies.

Case Studies

Three case studies follow. The first two point to the importance of aligning business strategy and key team results as the basis for developing team performance measures—a linkage promoted throughout this book. The third case demonstrates the transition from key results to performance measures—a cloudy transformation for many hard-to-measure teams.

Case Study: The Software Development Team

When this team first attempted to develop measures, it made virtually no progress because it did not have a team strategy or a clear understanding of the organization's business strategy. Following this initial failure, the team members had a series of meetings to answer the question, "We know we can do better, but how can we?"

Team TL43 is a team of eight software engineers who develop software for aerospace engineering applications. Their company, Cruise Technologies (a pseudonym), is a defense contractor that tests new rocket and airplane designs.

Cruise Tech's income breaks down into three categories: private contracts (10–15 percent), defense contracts (50–60 percent), and infrastructure projects—paid for by military funds (30–40 percent). Due to decreasing defense budgets, funds in category three are steadily diminishing. In addition, to compete for both private and defense contracts, Cruise Tech must reduce its operating costs. Employees affectionately refer to the business strategy as "Cheaper, Cheaper, Cheaper." Since completing contracts in less time also saves money, the strategy might be more accurately thought of as "Cheaper, Faster." Nevertheless, the strategy is crucial to the survival and future success of the organization.

Cruise Tech's external customers are also interested in reducing costs. One of the primary ways to realize savings is through reduced cycle time. Every day saved in the development of a new airplane saves a significant sum of money. In response to customer requests, via contracts, TL43 develops state-of-the-art computational software for data analysis and evaluation. In addition to improving the precision of computations, the software typically saves time for the user, therefore helping reduce cycle time.

TL43 was unclear on its team strategy in part because it was torn between satisfying its external customers, developing new customers, and helping its internal customers to reduce operating costs. Therefore, the team convened a series of meetings to determine its primary customer and to develop an appropriate team strategy. After much discussion, the team decided that its internal customer was its first priority, due to the company's need to reduce costs. It is important to note that the primary internal customer provides funding for TL43. Even as the internal customer was designated as primary, the team still wants to maintain and develop its relationship with external customers.

Along with determining its primary customer, the team strove to clarify its strategy. How could the team help its internal customer reduce costs while continuing to provide quality software solutions to the external customers? After much additional discussion, team members decided on the following strategy.

The team would review the entire range of projects for external customers and determine which of the software programs it had developed for external customers could also be used by internal customers. Since the software was developed with the goal of saving the external customer time and therefore money, some of those programs could also be used, with minor modifications, to save time and money for internal customers—thereby leveraging projects. This strategy differed from what the team had done in the past, which had a much more narrow focus: one or two team members would work on a given contract for an external customer in relative isolation from other team members and internal customers. In the new strategy, the team regularly discusses all its projects and looks for opportunities to use these new tools for its internal customer.

Looking back, the team members see that their former way of working was as individuals who did their own jobs without looking beyond the original application. In other words, they weren't truly working as a team. How they worked together might be pictured as in Figure 3.3.

Under the new strategy, the team members had to look across all the projects they were doing to find opportunities to leverage those tools to help their internal customer. Therefore, they all needed to know what the others were developing and what problems the internal customer had that their tools could solve. They also had to understand how the project schedule for the external customers could be modified to allow for tools to be adapted from those projects. This new strategy requires the team members to work together as a team, rather than a collection of individuals. Their new strategy states, "As a team, we will use a tool with as many people as possible and in as many ways as possible." A diagram of how they work together to make this happen might look like Figure 3.4.

Figure 3.3   Team TL43's Old Way of Working

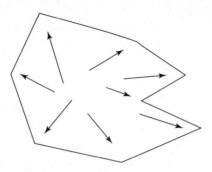

Figure 3.4   Team TL43's New Way of Working

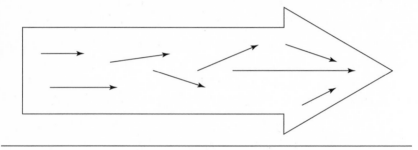

The software development team learned two valuable lessons during its strategy sessions. First, the team members learned they could work through a problem even though they were in conflict. Initially, the team disagreed severely about the team strategy. Some members wanted to serve only the external customers; some wanted to give the priority to the internal customer. Each side felt very strongly about its position. When the conflict began to get uncomfortable, the team almost gave up, just to keep the peace. However, one team member urged them to continue, and in about fifteen more minutes, they reached a resolution. Afterward, one team member said, "Often the solution can be found just past the point where you want to quit." The team found it could work through an uncomfortable situation successfully. This experience built the team's confidence.

The team also learned that it could look at the big picture; that is, it could take more of a managerial view rather than an employee's view. Before, the team members just focused on their individual projects, as employees typically do. Now they looked at the totality of their work and the opportunities to spin off software tools that could help their internal customer.

Given this new team strategy, performance measurement became much easier for the software development team. Aligning the business strategy of "Cheaper, Faster" and the team strategy of helping internal customers save time led to the key measure. This new measure was the number of new applications of their software adopted by internal customers. The work that the team did created an excellent line of sight between the business strategy, team strategy, and team measurement. This line of sight is shown in Figure 3.5.

Clearly, this team needs other measures of performance, but the measures will supplement this primary line of sight. Indeed, the team members chose a measure of the dollar value of the software tools leveraged from projects. This adds a quality dimension to the first measure. They also agreed on a measure of increases in the

Figure 3.5   Line of Sight for Team TL43

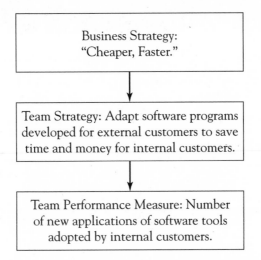

Business Strategy:
"Cheaper, Faster."

Team Strategy: Adapt software programs developed for external customers to save time and money for internal customers.

Team Performance Measure: Number of new applications of software tools adopted by internal customers.

customer base, which gives them a handle on how well they are doing with their external customers.

These three measures provide a good beginning to a measurement system for the software development team. Is it enough to fully capture the strategy? Probably not, but measurement systems rarely start out perfect. The team feels a need to further refine the measures. For instance, these three measures all track end results; they lack the capacity to capture cause and effect with regard to the team's strategy. If the strategy were to help the internal customer save time and money as measured by number of new software solutions adopted by internal customers, what would cause this to happen? This team is currently working on a diagram (Figure 3.6) to fully articulate the tactics within its strategy. After examining this diagram, team members will look for an additional measure that will tell them if they are taking the critical actions that will lead their internal customers to take advantage of the software solutions.

To execute its strategy, the team needs to acquire funding from its primary internal customer so it can enhance and modify the tools it develops for external customers. These enhanced and modified tools will benefit the external customers and can benefit internal customers. To apply these software tools internally, the team must

Figure 3.6   New Diagram for Team TL43

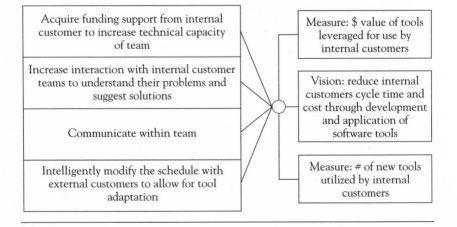

increase its interaction with the internal customer teams to understand their problems. Once Team TL43 understands those problems, it can offer the tools as solutions. To know what tools they have available, the team members need to communicate among themselves about the projects they are working on. They use an internal newsletter for this, as well as their team meetings. On some of the projects for external customers, the team members may need to negotiate a slight modification in the schedule so that the external customer gets what they want, and yet time is available to spin off a tool for an internal customer.

The team strategy received full approval by management, since it supports the organization's business strategy. The team performance measures track the team strategy fairly well, but the team sees room for improvement there. It also sees room for improvement in how to use its team measures for problem solving. Overall, this team is pleased with its team strategy. The members have a heightened sense of energy and a sense of taking charge of their own destiny. Moreover, they are now really working as a team, and they have answered the question of what they can do to improve.

Case Study: University Graduate Program

There are two issues working against performance measurement in universities: a culture of protection from accountability and a long-standing tradition of individualism for professors. If one accepts these two issues as real, then a university program would have to qualify as a hard-to-measure group.

An industrial and organizational psychology program embarked on an improvement effort that began with strategic planning and performance measurement. This group of eight faculty members reasoned that to meet the goal of becoming a nationally recognized master's level program, it had to do well in several areas. It needed to attract graduate students with high levels of ability and motivation. In addition, the faculty members needed to do a good job of teaching, publishing and presenting their work, interfacing with professional organizations and businesses, and acquiring resources from the university.

The professors reasoned that to become a top program required teamwork. This became a key component of their strategy. The other part of the strategy was to attract and select only the best students. In the past, the team had accepted all applicants to the graduate program who met the minimum criteria. This policy was consistent with the culture of the larger organization and made sense thirty years ago, when the program was first begun. At that time, the program needed students to justify hiring faculty, so it was reasonable to take large numbers of students by having low admission standards. Thirty years later, the same policy was in place. This had two results. First, the program was admitting more students than it could handle. Second, there was too much variability in the ability level of the students. This situation resulted in many long meetings on underperforming students and students who were not finishing the program in the allotted time. This was a major constraint in the team's performance. The dimensions of performance measurement shown in Table 3.1 align with the team's strategy and the major constraint just mentioned.

To develop the dimensions and measures of performance, the team held a series of meetings. The primary customers, the graduate students, were present in most of these meetings and often facilitated the discussions. Involving the customers in the measurement process helped the team to establish the proper perspective, and it created an air of honesty. Toward the end of the measurement process, the next three levels of administration reviewed the measurement system and provided feedback to the team.

Once these dimensions were determined, the team discussed the alignment between the dimensions and the strategic plan. Following this, the team brainstormed measures, compared them against criteria for good measures and decided on the sixteen measures shown in Table 3.2. The team members felt that sixteen measures were not too many, since they would only measure their performance once a year.

Table 3.1   Dimensions of Graduate Program Performance

Dimension	Definition	Importance
1. Primary customers (students)	Getting high-quality students—includes recruiting, selecting, training, retaining and placing graduate students	37 percent
2. Faculty productivity	Faculty doing their jobs well—includes research and student satisfaction with faculty	16 percent
3. Teamwork	Having team processes that function well—includes program evaluation, feedback, planning, collaboration, communication, values, role differentiation, decision making, and teamwork	15 percent
4. Resources	Having sufficient resources—includes equipment, personnel, space, time, materials, internal monetary support, student monetary support, and administrative support	15 percent
5. Outside activities	Interfacing with other important systems—includes student internships; public relations and public service by faculty; and consulting, professional activities, and professional presentations by faculty and students	17 percent

Once these measures were identified, performance standards and importance weights were applied to the measures to attain a composite score, a process that will be explained in Chapter Four. Following this work, one team member benchmarked the measures with similar programs in other universities. Those teams agreed that the proposed measures were appropriate, except for the teamwork measure. Academic programs rarely function as a team, but this program wanted to try the team concept. In addition to measures, importance weights and performance standards were also benchmarked with similar programs. Benchmarking was crucial, since there was no other way of verifying the measurement system.

Table 3.2 Measures of Graduate Program Performance

Dimension	Measure
Primary customers (students)	1. Average Graduate Record Exam of incoming students (Quantitative plus Analytical) 2. Average Grade Point Average of incoming students 3. Average comprehensive exam score 4. Selection Ratio: Number new students accepted/number applied 5. Student and alumni satisfaction survey
Faculty productivity	6. Average number of publications/year 7. Average number of conference papers and presentations/year 8. Four questions on faculty from student satisfaction survey
Teamwork	9. Teamwork survey
Resources	10. Graduate student/faculty ratio 11. Internal grants and release time 12. Number of assistantships/fellowships 13. Faculty satisfaction with university resources survey
Outside activities	14. Professional involvement of students 15. Professional involvement of faculty 16. Number of paid internships and number of students or faculty involved in consulting projects each semester, totaled for year

Once the measurement system was complete and verified, one team member collected data on each measure and fed that data into a spreadsheet to create a feedback report like the one shown in Table 3.3. Data were collected once a year and discussed in a team meeting in the spring. After discussion, the team decided to raise its admission standards and take a smaller number of students. This policy received administrative approval and was enacted in 1994, and it resulted in improved performance. Note that in Table 3.3 the

Table 3.3   Example Feedback Report for the Graduate Program

Dimension/Measure	Raw Score	Effectiveness Score	Percent of Maximum
Student			
Average GRE (Q + A)	1134	8.3	92 percent
Average GPA	3.25	3.8	48 percent
Average Comps	86.6	0.0	100 percent
Selection Ratio	0.39	4.5	45 percent
Student Survey	5.3	3.2	35 percent
Faculty			
Number of Publications	5.5	0.5	10 percent
Number of Presentations	32	5.0	100 percent
Faculty Survey	5.78	2.2	36 percent
Teamwork			
Team Questionnaire	3.04	4.9	32 percent
Resources			
Student/Faculty Ratio	4.38	4.0	100 percent
Grants/Release Time	23	4.0	100 percent
Number of GTAs or Fellowships	15	1.0	25 percent
Faculty Satisfaction	4.32	0.0	0 percent
Outside Activities			
Student Involvement	3.3846	3.5	69 percent
Faculty Involvement	4.875	3.0	61 percent
Consulting Projects or Internships	69	7.0	100 percent
Overall Effectiveness		54.8	

selection ratio (number of students accepted divided by number of students applying) was 0.39. It was 1.0 in 1991 and 1992. A better selection ratio resulted in higher Graduate Record Exam scores and higher Grade Point Averages of incoming students. The team no longer had long meetings about underperforming students—because the students were now virtually all high performers.

Initially, this team discussed its performance and made improvements in admissions and recruiting. However, it stumbled on the issue of mutual accountability for its own performance. In 1995 and 1996, team members found they could not discuss areas of low performance if the cause was internal to the team. So low performance in faculty publications and teamwork became taboo topics in team meetings (see Table 3.3). This inability to discuss internal issues led to problems in team dynamics and an eventual drop in performance, as seen in Figure 3.7. During this time, the faculty quit having regular team meetings and no longer discussed its performance measures.

As in most organizations with no culture of accountability, it is likely that this team never truly wanted accountability. Therefore, when performance problems were identified, it wasn't committed enough to the process to work through those problems. In the absence of pressure from the organization for accountability, the team retreated to a traditional posture of individualism rather than teamwork. While this was a hard-to-measure team, the primary issues were the organizational culture and individual beliefs about performance, rather than measurement per se.

Case Study: The Internal Consulting Team

External consultants helping internal consultants adopt innovative management practices is a novel twist. Such was the case in the Operations Division of a major telecommunications company.

Figure 3.7   Graduate Program Performance

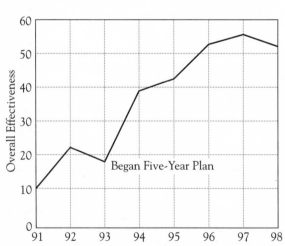

Anticipating competitive pressure as a result of deregulation, the Corporate Productivity Department sought assistance from a consulting firm for whom one of the authors served as a senior consultant. The assistant vice president for operations planning had developed a strong appreciation for the pivotal role performance measurement plays in the improvement process. As a result, the internal consulting group (composed largely of applied statisticians, operations research scientists, and industrial psychologists) decided to develop measures at the department, district, and section levels. This case study reports on the development of department measures that provided and tracked expectations that unified all districts and sections.

The external consultant guided the senior department managers through the Total Measurement Development process described as Method 6 earlier in this chapter. First, department vision, mission, and strategy statements were developed in concert with corporate strategy to help the team identify what it wanted to accomplish (Strategic Self-View). Interestingly enough, the department essentially aimed to demonstrate the same practices it desired to see its internal customers exhibit (strategic planning, performance measurement, team problem solving, recognition, and so on). Second, three tiers of customers stratified by level of importance were identified (see Exhibit 3.2). Based on the belief that an acceptable methodology for analyzing customer needs was not readily available and given the team members' related skills, the team decided to use its own customer value questionnaire (Customer View). Third, the department's manager, the assistant vice president, and his superior were interviewed regarding their expectations for the team (Accountability View). Not surprisingly, given the way these managers took the lead in the "white-collar improvement initiative," their responses were very consistent with the team's own view of the desired accomplishments: model expected behavior, provide consulting support, and customers will demonstrate the practices that will result in valuable performance gains. Last, the team reviewed the existing performance data used at the

---

Exhibit 3.2   Department Customer List

The following customers were stratified into three tiers based on their number of current contacts with the department and the desired rate of such "moments of truth." Tier A contains those customers to whom the department would like to devote most of its efforts and services, Tier C the least.

Tier A

- Executive officers
- Department heads and the employees in
  - Budgets
  - Customer Services
  - Network Services
- Marketing
- Corporate and Regional Personnel

Tier B

- Engineering
- Material
- Union
- Real Estate
- Corporate Performance
- Other telephone companies (under service agreements)
- Comptrollers
- Administrative Services

Tier C

- Law
- Finance
- Network
- Medical
- Purchasing
- Other companies
- Public Relations

---

departmental level and within districts (Information Systems View). This consisted primarily of budget reports and logs of internal consulting services (contacts, project hours, and so on).

The responses generated by the four views clustered around ten key results or products. Table 3.4 lists these results, their business or customer requirements, and the corresponding measures that were selected. The team specified the calculations and identified the sources of data required by each measure. At the time of the external consultant's departure, the department team as well as district teams

Table 3.4 Corporate Productivity Department Results, Requirements, and Measures

Result	*Requirement*	*Measure*
1. Strategic plans developed	• Quality, Timeliness	• Percent of strategic plans approved by target date. Approval is assumed to address the quality requirement insofar as it would be contingent on meeting predetermined criteria such as identification of customer needs, strengths and weaknesses, and so on.
2. Productivity and quality initiatives started	• Quantity, Quality, Cost	• Percent of division employees affected. • Ratio of consulting hours provided to hours in plan (total and by project).
3. Employee involvement practices started	• Quantity, Quality	• Percent of division employees participating. • Average score on "employee involvement" survey administered across division.
4. Measurement plans implemented	• Quantity, Quality	• Percent of targeted units/teams with scorecards. • Percent of plans with minimum score on measurement plan checklist (that is, percent passing).
5. Division managers' awareness of department services established	• Quantity	• Percent of managers attending service briefings who contact department for additional information or assistance.
6. Assessments conducted	• Quality, Cost, Timeliness	• Percent of recommendations accepted for implementation. • Actual versus planned hours. • Percent completed on schedule.

Table 3.4 Corporate Productivity Department Results, Requirements, and Measures (*Continued*)

Result	Requirement	Measure
7. Division manager knowledge and skills in select concepts and methods acquired	• Quality, Cost	• Percent reduction in consulting hours post training. • Actual versus planned training costs per employee.
8. Department staff knowledge and skills in select concepts and methods acquired	• Quantity, Quality, Cost	• Percent of staff completing planned training hours (as specified in annual individual development plan). • Annual customer ratings on "center of competence" survey. • Actual versus planned total training costs.
9. Quality of service reports delivered	• Timeliness	• Percent of reports (internal and external) delivered on time
10. Corporate policy and strategy statements influenced	• Quantity	• Productivity Department rating of executive pronouncements (degree of consistency with desired practices: 1–10 scale).

were reviewing the measures on at least a monthly basis, more frequently at the district team level. Measurable goals were set on some of the measures perceived to be the most meaningful, and problem solving and process improvement activities to reduce the gap between actual and expected levels of performance had just begun. Several measures were discarded, a clear sign that feedback was occurring.

In summary, the Total Measurement Development Method forced the department to ask some tough questions about what constituted valuable performance. It provided a way to translate the white-collar productivity mission into meaningful measures that could be reviewed and used to drive improvement. Most important, the high involvement used throughout the process clarified the team's purpose and fostered ownership for meeting expectations.

Recommendations for Hard-to-Measure Teams

Hard-to-measure teams present a unique opportunity to hone the team skills of all involved. It is not so much that such teams defy measurement as that they challenge the measurement process to truly help them improve their performance and work life. In our experience, it's possible to develop a family of measures for any team. We have provided instructive lessons, structured methods, and illustrative cases to support this contention. However, dragging team members through the measurement process to develop a set of measures that the team will not use is not only a waste of effort, it is also likely to damage team functioning. To avoid such a pitfall, we suggest reminding teams that the fundamental intent is to use measures as the basis for reinforcing noteworthy accomplishments on one hand, and driving performance improvement activities on the other. In addition, we offer the following recommendations:

- *Employ a high-involvement approach throughout the process.* Hard-to-measure teams test the patience of team members and tempt management to take shortcuts to get the measurement process rolling. Given the level of resistance to measurement typical of these teams, this would be a fatal mistake. The often ambiguous nature of the work performed by these teams also necessitates their involvement from beginning to end.

- *Establish a line of sight between business strategy and the team's measures*. This fosters two benefits: it ensures that the team's results contribute to competitive advantage, and it provides an opportunity for the team to develop and commit to its own strategy. The team will want to see how successful the strategy is, capturing at least the team members' curiosity about the related role of the measurement system. The curiosity eventually will be replaced by the ongoing benefits associated with measurement, feedback, and subsequent performance improvement activities. It is best if the business strategy is communicated directly to the team by management, in person, to allow for questions and answers.

- *If the hard-to-measure team is more a collection of independent performers than a team, consider redesigning the structure of the team*. The redesign can simply consist of developing a strategy that promotes interdependence among team members, as the software development team did. It might also involve changing team boundaries so that individuals find themselves in groups with those having a common purpose or function, or it may mean changing jobs within the team's boundaries to establish a unified focus. An excellent example of such redesign at Blue Cross and Blue Shield was recently published (Alonso, 1999). In this case study, the results indicated significant improvement in measures of customer service as a result of redesigning the work to increase team-member interdependence and customer focus. Readers interested in more about team design are also referred to a useful book by Susan Mohrman and associates (Mohrman, Cohen, & Mohrman, 1995).

- *Select the measurement development method that best matches your current situation and needs*. If the business requires a fast rate of improvement and resources are scarce, the team should probably not elect to use the Total Measurement Development process. The Menu Selection method would be a more appropriate alternative. However, if the team's mission and desired accomplishments are vague, several attempts at developing measures have already failed, and the organization wishes to establish high-involvement practices, the holistic model is a good fit.

- *Do something.* Regardless of the method the team employs, it is important to get started. Don't insist on precise or comprehensive systems with hard-to-measure teams. An incomplete measurement system that the team uses for problem solving is far better than a complete system that is not used. For instance, if the team successfully solves problems using just one measure, this experience will probably lead to a search for additional measures. If the team members complain that the system is incomplete, that's a good sign. The sophistication of the measurement system should not exceed the commitment of the team to use it.

- *Involve customers in the measurement development process.* Invite customers to the meetings to help identify both desired results and customer requirements (quantity, quality, cost, timeliness). Involving customers gets the team outside itself and affords a more objective perspective on performance. A strong team-customer relationship can do a lot to break down resistance and other barriers to measurement. However, remember to balance customer requirements with business requirements. Teams can get into trouble, for instance, if they attempt to provide high-quality products or services without regard to cost.

- *Allow enough time for hard-to-measure teams to develop measures.* The difficulties are well documented, so be realistic. Don't attempt to develop a measurement system during periods of high demand. Performance measures are part of a new lifestyle for teams. However, a team can't work on a new lifestyle if what it needs is surgery. Get the crises out of the way first, then spend the necessary time to develop new habits like measuring your team's performance.

Assessing Your Team

1. Pick a hard-to-measure team. Analyze why it is hard to measure using the lessons learned at the beginning of this chapter to stimulate your thinking.

2. Identify the records and other end products that are currently collected that reflect the work performed by the team you chose. Examine and categorize the reports, logs, and so on. What are some potential measures of the team's performance based on this documentation?

3. Summarize the strategy for this team. For help with this activity, complete the strategic self-view as described in Step 2 of the Total Measurement Development method. In addition, review the software development team and undergraduate graduate program case studies with special attention to the team strategy.

4. Talk to the customers of this team. What are their expectations for each of the products or services they receive?

5. Talk to the manager responsible for the team as well as the manager at the next highest level. What are their performance expectations for the team? For help, answer the questions in the accountability view—Step 4 of the Total Measurement Development method.

6. Based on the team strategy, customer needs, and management expectations, identify one or two key performance measures for this team. How would the team respond to feedback on these measures? What would be the level of commitment to solving problems and improving processes based on these measures? How would the team react to starting with a few measures as opposed to a more complete measurement system?

Chapter Four

Seeing the Big Picture

Integrating the Measurement System into a Composite Score

Two managers are talking:

> *George:* It seems like we're drowning in numbers. I wish we could find some way to reduce the amount of information we have to deal with. I'm mostly interested in the big picture, unless there's a problem.
>
> *Peter:* Yeah, I know, but I still want to be able to get more information in areas where we need to improve, or when we want to understand exactly what we're doing well.

In this age of information overload, simplicity has a certain appeal. Wouldn't it be nice if you could have a measure that would give you the big picture and yet still give you the details when you need them? An index of group performance could provide the big picture, while the individual measures of team performance could indicate areas of strength and areas needing improvement. Then a team could "zoom in" on the areas needing improvement to get further details for problem solving. This would give the team and managers a system that simplifies the performance data yet gives them the details when they need it.

What does it take to get the composite score? By adding two more steps to the measurement process—importance weighting and setting performance standards—the performance-measurement system can create a composite score that yields the big picture. (Expect to add about one or two extra meetings to the development process.) Usually, the judgments about relative importance and performance standards are made anyway as a team initiates improvement efforts, so developing a composite score for the measurement system does not add much work. It does put all of the judgments about performance together in one place—the team's performance measurement system. Once the importance weights and performance standards are determined, the composite score can be obtained.

Advantages of a Composite Score

Why add a composite score to the measurement system? Here are five advantages we have learned from fifteen years of experience working with composite scores.

1.   *Performance-based pay for teams is much easier to understand and administer if the incentive is based on a single composite score of team performance.* When the composite score is in a percent format, the performance pay can simply be the composite score as a percent of the bonus pool. For example, a composite score of 25 would earn the team 25 percent of the bonus pool. The calculation of incentive pay should be perfectly transparent to the team members. They should be able to make their own calculations and confirm the payouts. A composite score makes this possible and eliminates the need for a separate system for the calculation of performance pay.

2.   *Valuable conversations can occur on the questions of what measures are most important and what the standards of performance should be.* In fact, this presents one of the best opportunities to get added value from the measurement process. For instance, many team members have developed insights into the business by listening to managers discuss why a particular level of performance on a measure is critical for the business's success. For team members to become business partners, they need to engage in these kinds of conversations.

3.   *The hallmark of a high-performance team is a consistently high level of performance or an improving trend in performance.* In

contrast, an erratic pattern with a low overall level of performance tells a different story. Managers benefit from the composite score because they can see the patterns of their teams' performance. Team members benefit because the composite score condenses information and provides them with a quick, easy gauge of their progress. Figure 4.1 demonstrates this point using an assembly team. In 1999, this team began using its measurement system for problem solving and improvement.

As a composite score, the GPI (Group Performance Index) tells the team how it is doing overall. Note how the composite score communicates the team's consistency and improvement compared to the preceding year. As one team member put it: "To get our incentive, all we have to do is keep this year's line above last year's line." It is motivating for teams to see how well they are doing overall. In a world overflowing with information, it is worth a great deal to point to a graph containing a single line that depicts the team's progress.

Figure 4.1   Overall Performance of the Assembly Team

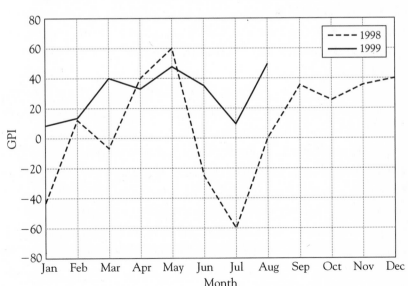

4. *Many business decisions are trade-offs.* When a team does have to make trade-offs, the team and management want to know if they made the right ones. Correct decisions will improve the composite score.

5. *Managers want considerable input on the importance weights of the measures and the performance standards.* This is important. Getting their fingerprints on the measurement system in this way gains valuable buy-in from management.

Valuable as it is, a composite score is optional. A team can have a good measurement system without it. The important thing is how the team uses its measurement system. The Xerox case study in Chapter Five is a good example; this team uses its measurement system very effectively without a composite score.

Disadvantages of a Composite Score

The main disadvantage of a composite score is the extra layer of complexity it creates in the measurement system. On the one hand, this additional layer of complexity requires some time to establish and understand. On the other hand, this process has been streamlined considerably in recent years with the use of computers and software like Microsoft Excel. Teams can now understand the composite score with a single training session.

The second disadvantage of a composite score concerns the way it partially compensates for variability in performance on the individual measures. Since performance on individual measures is summed in the composite, low performance on one measure can be offset, somewhat, by high performance on another measure. However, experience has shown that when a team has low performance on a measure, it will focus its improvement efforts on that measure even when the composite score is more positive.

Probably the greatest potential disadvantage with composite scores occurs when teams compare their composite scores to one another. If not managed, these comparisons can create excessive competition between teams. On the one hand, if teams need to cooperate and have no measures of cooperation built into the measurement system, the organization may suffer when the teams compete. On the other hand, some competition between teams can be very productive, especially when they share a common measure that requires cooperation.

Methods for Constructing a Composite Score

To create a composite score, different units (dollars, percentages, hours, or whatever) must be converted to a common denominator. There are three proven methods of developing a composite score: percent of goal accomplished, OMax (Oregon Matrix), and ProMES for Teams. This book advocates either percent of goal accomplished or ProMES for Teams but will try to provide an objective coverage for each method. Some team practitioners have requested a method for converting team performance measures to dollar values. While a proven method does not currently exist, it is possible. This chapter will address how performance measures could be converted to dollar values to create a composite score.

Percent of Goal Accomplished

The percent of goal accomplished is the most straightforward method. Goals can be easily established for each of a team's measures. Performance on each measure can then be expressed in terms of percent of goal accomplished, and those percents can be averaged as in Table 4.1.

Table 4.1   Using Percent of Goal as a Composite Score

Measure	Score	Percent of Goal	Goal
Productivity ($ per hour)	650	81	800
Quality (percent pass inspection)	92	93	99
On-time delivery (percent delivered on time)	57	57	100
Training (hours per employee)	10	25	40
Overall score (average)		64	

The composite score shows this team performing at 64 percent of its goal (on the average). The team has two obvious areas of improvement: timely delivery and training. Notice how low performance in these two areas is partially offset by high performance in quality and productivity. If the organization uses a pay-for-performance system, would the team qualify for 64 percent of the available bonus? Probably not, because it is so far below the goals in timely delivery and training.

The solution is to add an additional column for a threshold or minimum acceptable level of performance above which the team would be paid. The team does not get any score in the Percent of Goal column unless it passes the threshold. This additional column adds another level of complexity, because it requires judgments about how performance will be paid on each measure. More commonly, goals are set yearly and short-term targets are set quarterly or monthly as in the example in Table 4.2.

If the organization uses a team incentive, what effect will that have on a system like this? Except for high-performance teams, most teams will put downward pressure on the goals. The lower the goals, the higher the composite score and the greater the incentive. This downward pressure on goals does not establish a good foundation for improving team performance.

Table 4.2   Adding Thresholds and Targets to Percent of Goal Accomplished

Measure	Score	Percent of Goal	Threshold	Target	Goal
Productivity ($ per hour)	650	81	400	700	800
Quality (percent pass inspection)	92	93	80	95	99
On-time delivery (percent delivered on time)	57	0	80	90	100
Training (hours per employee)	10	0	20	30	40
Overall score (average)		43.5			

The alternative is for all of the goals to be set by upper management. This can work, especially if the teams participate in setting short-term goals—or at least decide how they will achieve the goals. Often, goals that are set at higher levels fail to motivate teams, because teams believe the goals are arbitrary or unrealistic. Managers may accept the goals, but team members often do not buy in unless they fully accept the rationale behind the goals. Such rationale usually comes from benchmarking with other teams, either internal or external to the company, or through dialogue with managers and customers at the team level.

OMax

Glen Felix and James Riggs of Oregon State University developed the OMax, also called the Oregon Matrix or the Objectives Matrix (Felix & Riggs, 1983). The OMax procedures have been widely used in a variety of organizations for the purpose of creating composite scores. The original Felix and Riggs procedure is still in use, but it has been updated by Craig Heninger (1994), also of Oregon State University. Using the Objectives Matrix, a team assigns an importance weight to each of its measures with the weights totaling 100. The team also sets a percent of milestone, or goal level, for each measure, such that the baseline (where the team is now) performance level equals 0 percent and performance at the long-range goal level equals 100 percent. This procedure produces a composite score that can reach 100, but, more commonly, ranges from 10 to 50. Table 4.3 presents an example of the Objectives Matrix.

Close examination of this matrix reveals that the team's performance scores are in the score column (third from the right). For the team's first measure, number of loans serviced, it had a raw score of 66. This converts to 40 percent of the goal for this measure, as per the top row. The 40 percent times the importance weight of 15 produces a value (weighted score) of 6, which reflects the team's percent of goal accomplished. In a similar fashion, each performance level on each measure converts to a percent-of-goal figure,

Table 4.3   Sample OMax for a Financial Services Team

Productivity Criteria	Baseline 0 percent	10 percent	20 percent	30 percent	40 percent	50 percent	60 percent	70 percent	80 percent	90 percent	Goal 100 percent	Score	Weight	Value
Loans serviced Department hours	30	39	48	57	[66]	75	84	93	102	111	120	66	15	6
Late computer reports 22 days	90	81	72	63	54	45	36	27	18	9	[0]	0	5	5
Manual coupons Payments received	4	7	10	13	16	19	22	[25]	28	32	36	25	10	7
Policy errors # of new policies	29.0	22.0	16.0	11.0	7.0	4.0	[2.0]	1.0	0.75	0.50	0.25	2	20	12
# of inquiries Loans serviced	0.90	0.80	0.72	[0.64]	0.56	0.48	0.40	0.32	0.24	0.16	0.09	.64	15	5
Investor complaints Commercial loans	8.7	7.9	7.1	6.3	5.5	[4.7]	3.9	3.1	2.3	1.5	0.8	4.7	30	15
Hours missed Department hours	11.0	10.2	9.9	8.8	7.7	6.6	5.5	4.4	[3.3]	2.2	1.2	3.3	5	4
Total													100	54

Source: Craig Heninger, *Performance by Criteria Matrix.* Corvallis, OR: Heninger, 1994. Used by permission of Craig Heninger.

which is then multiplied by the importance weight. The composite score (54 in this case) is the sum of the weighted scores (the last column), indicating the team reached 54 percent of its goal. The best the team could possibly score is 100.

This OMax example demonstrates how a family of measures can be integrated into a composite score. A team could track each of the measures as well as the composite over time. From this information, the team can see how it is doing on each measure and how it is doing overall. The key judgments the team has to make are the importance weights and the corresponding goal level for each performance level. The judgments required to develop the composite scores are slightly more complex than for the percent-of-goal method, but they are equally subject to the downward pressure on goals by teams.

In contrast to percent of goal accomplished, the OMax provides a score for team members, even if they do not reach the goal. Therefore, the team can get some incentive, even if it does not completely achieve its goal.

ProMES for Teams

In the mid-1980s, Pritchard and associates (1988) developed a different method for creating a composite score. Pritchard's method, called ProMES (Productivity Measurement and Enhancement System; see Pritchard, 1990, 1995), has seen considerable acceptance in Europe but less in the United States. Jones and associates have simplified the method and called it ProMES for Teams (Jones, Buerkle, Hall, Rupp, & Matt, 1993; Jones & Moffett, 1998). ProMES for Teams has been used with a wide variety of manufacturing and service teams in the United States.

ProMES for Teams has three objectives: choose the right measures by linking the team's measurement system closely to the needs of the customer and the organization's business strategy; involve the team in development of the measurement system, so it will understand the system and have ownership of it; and allow incentives to be easily added to the system in a way that is understandable to teams.

The ProMES for Teams approach uses the following steps to create the composite score.

1. *Determine the dimensions of team performance.* These dimensions are important areas (sometimes called key results areas) in which the team must do well in order to be effective. Dimensions provide a map of the work domain. Typical dimensions are productivity, cost control, quality, customer service, training, teamwork, sales, growth, and so on. The final set of dimensions is a blend of the important areas of team performance, as determined by the team, management, and the customers. For example, this process produced a set of dimensions for the assembly team consisting of quality, productivity, cycle time, on-time shipments, and assembly start. The assembly team could have added safety and training as two additional dimensions, but these five were thought to be the most important.

2. *The dimensions are weighted for importance.* For example, if the organization's values say that quality is job one, then the dimension of quality—or its most important cause—should have the greatest weight. To determine the weights, each team member divides 100 points among the dimensions. These points are then averaged across team members for each dimension. Management reviews these weights and may set limits within which they can vary. Customers influence the weights by virtue of the importance they place on certain areas of team performance (for example, quality or delivery time). The dimension weights for an assembly team might be as follows: Quality, 35 percent; Productivity, 10 percent; On-Time Shipments, 25 percent; Cycle Time, 15 percent; Assembly Start, 15 percent. These dimensions and their associated importance weights reflect the business strategy and the team strategy. The business strategy is to respond quickly to customer orders and to be the low-cost provider. The team strategy is to do the job right the first time and to get the materials team members need to start the assembly job on time. Based on this strategy, the team

weighted Quality as most important (35 percent). Responsiveness is addressed by On-Time Shipments (25 percent) and Cycle Time (15 percent). Note that the Assembly Start dimension reflects the team strategy of getting the material to start the jobs on time. Productivity is the least important, because productivity results from doing well in the other four areas. For this team, productivity is plantwide and requires cooperation between teams.

3. *One or more measures are determined for each dimension.* Ideas for these measures originate with the members of the organization and the customers. The team may select measures from a menu of possible measures provided to them by management or a steering committee. Ideally, most of the measures the team needs are already collected by the organization. The team may have to make adjustments to the preexisting measures so as to isolate the portion over which it has control. Alternatively, team members may brainstorm a list of possible measures, then select the most appropriate ones using a set of criteria for good measures.

4. *If there is only one measure per dimension, the dimension weight becomes the importance weight for that one measure within that dimension.* For the assembly team example, the importance weights of the measures are the same as the importance weights for the dimensions. In cases where there is more than one measure per dimension, the team assigns importance weights to each measure by dividing 100 points across the measures within each dimension. The measure weights are then multiplied by the dimension weight to obtain the final set of measure weights for that dimension. For example, in one chemical processing team, the quality dimension had three measures: press utilization, batches reblended, and batches doctored. The measure weights were 75, 20, and 5, respectively. These figures were multiplied by the quality dimension weight (0.50) to get the final set of measure weights: (75 * 0.50 = 37.5, 20 * 0.50 = 10, and 5 * 0.50 = 2.5) for the quality dimension.

5. *Once the final importance weights have been established, the measures can be integrated into the composite index.* To create the composite, the team determines the performance standards

for each measure. In consultation with management, the team determines the best possible case, the worst possible case, and the minimally acceptable level of performance for each measure. The best case may be the goal, a benchmark, or merely a judgment agreed on by the team and management. The worst case is usually determined by historical data. The minimally acceptable level is defined as the point that identifies a problem may be beginning, such as a lower control limit in statistical process control. These judgments are displayed graphically in relation to the importance weights for the measure. This graphic display is called a *contingency*, and it represents performance standards. The contingency is the relationship between performance on a particular measure and the effectiveness of the team. The contingency translates the raw score of the measure into an effectiveness score. Since each measure is weighted for importance, the team can only be as effective on the measure as that measure is important. The contingency for the productivity measure of the assembly team is given in Figure 4.2. Note that the vertical axis only goes to 10 and −10, which reflects the importance weight of the measure (the weight for productivity is 10 percent). The horizontal axis reflects possible values

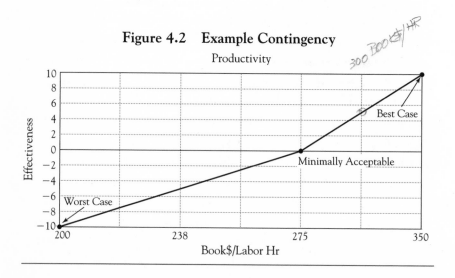

Figure 4.2 Example Contingency
Productivity

of the measure. The sloping line represents the relationship between the measure and team effectiveness. The sloping line is determined by the judgments about best case, worst case, and min‐imally acceptable levels of performance. For instance, the team is maximally effective when it produces $350 book dollars per labor hour and minimally acceptable when it produces $275 book dollars per hour. The worst‐case scenario for productivity is to drop to $200 book dollars per hour. If the team produced $300 book dollars per hour for a month, it would receive an effectiveness score of 5. Note that the performance standards are based on the same unit of time for which performance will be measured. In other words, if the team intends to measure its performance each month, the perfor‐mance standard is based on a monthly average.

All measures have contingencies, so each measure can be trans‐lated into a common denominator and summed into a composite, called the Group Performance Index (GPI). The team can then receive feedback on a sheet like the one shown in Table 4.4. Dimensions and importance weights are set in italics with measures just below. The monthly performance data is in column two.

Table 4.4   ProMES for Teams Example Feedback Sheet

Assembly Team Performance	*Data*	*Effectiveness*	*Goal*
Quality (35 percent)			
Defects per unit	.40	−17.5	.15
Productivity (10 percent)			
Book$ per labor hour	$300	5.00	$350
Cycle time (15 percent)			
Average cycle time in days	12.5	15.00	12.5
On‐time shipments (25 percent)			
Percent jobs finished on schedule	89	7.50	95
Assembly start (15 percent)			
Percent jobs set up when scheduled	75	7.50	85
Group performance index		17.50	

The effectiveness translation is in column three. For example, the productivity score of 300 has an effectiveness score of 5 as determined from the contingency in Figure 4.2. The goals, an optional column, are in column four. If this team had a pay-for-performance system, each team member would earn 17.5 percent of the bonus pool. The bonus pool, in this case, was funded by the productivity measure, and the plant had to reach a target of 6 percent improvement to fund the bonus system.

In addition to the feedback sheet, the team receives graphs of each measure over time, so the members can assess trends. They also receive more detailed information for problem solving, such as type and date of defects.

Which Method to Use?

Percent of goal accomplished or ProMES for Teams are both preferred methods for creating a composite score. They each require judgments concerning performance standards and will give a composite score on which incentives can be paid. The primary difference is that ProMES for Teams accounts for performance on measures that are below the minimally acceptable measure by applying negative scores. The percent-of-goal method does not use negative scores. Any performance below the threshold level just receives a zero in its contribution to the composite score. This makes ProMES for Teams more precise, but most teams will find the percent-of-goal method easier to understand. So we recommend ProMES for Teams when there is a concern for accounting for performance that might fall below standards. We recommend the percent-of-goal method when the goal is ease of understanding. However, if team incentives will be used, the percent-of-goal method frequently results in downward pressure on the goals during goal setting. So care must be taken in setting goals. As for OMax, it parallels ProMES and can be used in the same situations, but the output provided is more complex.

Dollar Values

From time to time, team practitioners express an interest in converting a family of team measures to dollar values. Converting all of a team's measures to dollar values entails a costly procedure. However, it can be done. A few organizations may require dollar values because they want to know the return on investment in teams.

Measures such as productivity, cost savings, and lost-time accidents, which are already in dollar form, are easy to convert into the composite. Measures such as scrap and time-savings can be converted to dollar form by multiplying the unit cost by the number of units. More difficult to compute are measures such as defects and customer returns, because they include lost opportunity costs as well as labor and materials. A higher level of judgment is required for these types of measures. For instance, what is the dollar value of 85 percent on-time delivery, 95 percent customer satisfaction, or 70 percent training requirements met?

A group of experts, usually consisting of managers, engineers, and accountants, can make a series of judgments about the dollar value of different levels of performance on measures of this type. Whoever is requesting the dollar figures for team performance should be in this group, since they will be the consumers of the information. After making the judgments, the group can assign a confidence level, given as a percentage, to the judgments for each measure. For instance, if the group agrees that 85 percent on-time delivery is worth $10,000, it can multiply this judgment by the confidence factor to derive a value. For example, suppose the factor was 60 percent. This would result in a worth of $6,000 for reaching 85 percent on-time delivery. Factoring in the confidence of the judgments makes the procedure more conservative and generally more acceptable to managers. Once the dollar values are determined, they can be related to the performance just as you would with the percent of goal, ProMES for Teams, or OMax methods.

Jack Phillips of the Performance Resources Organization has perfected a method of using judgments from subject matter experts to convert performance improvements to dollar value (Phillips, 1991, 1995). Most of Dr. Phillips's work focuses on evaluating the Return on Investment (ROI) of training programs. He admits that the procedure is labor intensive and recommends that it should be used for a 10 percent sample of a company's training programs.

Summary

Most performance measurement systems can benefit from creating a composite score. The composite score tells the team and management how well the team is doing overall. It is particularly helpful to see this trend across time. Attaching incentives to measurement systems is easier with a composite score. We recommend either the percent-of-goal method or the ProMES for Teams method for creating a composite score.

Assessing Your Team

Complete each of these items based on the measures you identified in Chapter Two and the strategies you developed in Chapter One.

1. Apply importance weights to each dimension by dividing 100 points among them. Draw a pie chart showing the relative size of each dimension.

2. List your dimensions in Table 4.5. For each dimension, identify one or two measures. For the purpose of this example, keep the total number of measures to six or less.

Table 4.5 Performance Dimensions, Measures, and Importance Weights

Dimension	Measure	Weight

3. Determine the importance weight for each measure. If you have more than one measure per dimension, divide 100 points among the measures within each dimension, then multiply the measure weight by the dimension weight. Put this value in percent format. Complete the weight column in Table 4.5.

4. Determine best case, worst case, and minimally acceptable level of performance for each measure, and post your answers in Table 4.6.

Table 4.6 Performance Standards for ProMES for Teams

Measure	Worst Case	Minimally Acceptable	Best Case

5. Draw a contingency graph for each measure.

   a. Begin by filling in the vertical axis using the importance weight of the measure as the top value, and then place a negative importance weight as the lowest value.

   b. Fill in the horizontal axis by using the worst case for the measure as the lowest value and the best case as the highest value. Mark the value for the minimally acceptable level in its place on the horizontal axis. Make tick marks for intermediate values.

   c. Mark the three points on the line graph where the best case, worst case, and minimally acceptable values fall. Draw lines connecting the points. For this example, draw a contingency graph for each measure that you identified. (Your graphs should resemble the one in Figure 4.2.)

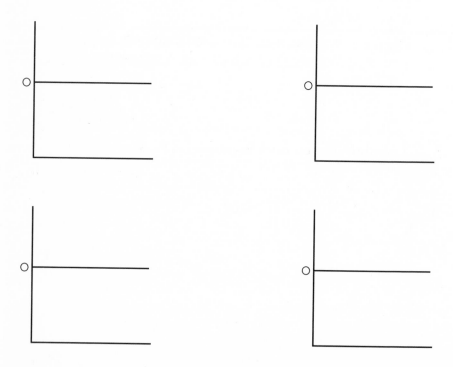

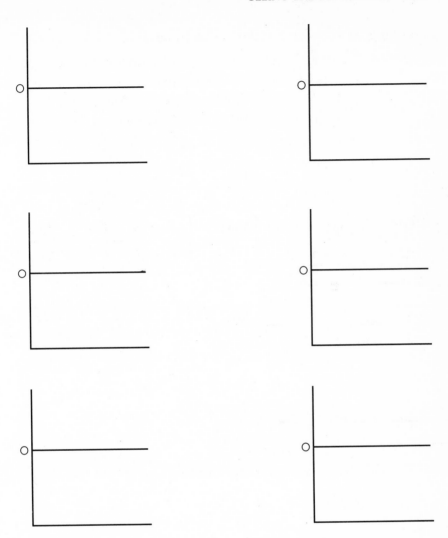

6. Alternative—Percent of Goal Method:

   a. Determine the long-term goal, short-term target, and threshold level for each measure. The threshold level is the same as the minimally acceptable level in Activity 4. This is the point below which performance is clearly unacceptable.

   b. Put these values in Table 4.7.

Table 4.7   Performance Standards for Percent of Goal Method

Measure	Threshold	Target	Goal

Chapter Five

Team Members as Business Partners

Xerox Corporation

By Tressa Cherry

This case study presents how members of a typical service team in a large corporation evolved from dissatisfied low-performers to high performers who take pride in their performance and accomplishments as a team. It offers insight into the development of the team's self-awareness and the subsequent trials and growth that followed. Special emphasis is placed on how the team members use their performance measures. This case study reflects the opinions and experiences of members of Team 47, not necessarily those of Xerox Corporation.

Everyone has heard the story of the high-performing team leading the way in an organization, acting as business partners rather than employees. To the typical worker, such high performance can seem to be the furthest thing from day-to-day reality. What processes are required for a team to achieve this level of performance? This is a case study of one team that rose to such heights.

This is an important case because it *is* about a typical team of people that somehow became atypical. Close examination of these team members' evolution reveals critical points in their paths where certain questions, decisions, or behaviors motivated them to be where they are today. This case is descriptive in nature rather than prescriptive. However, Team 47's critical points of progress can be useful landmarks, and its subsequent choices at each point could be useful discussion topics for any team interested in growth toward higher performance.

Background

Today the eight service technicians who make up Team 47—also known as the Hi-Rockers—form one of the teams leading the way in the Xerox Corporation. In 1997, Xerox bestowed the prestigious X-Team Award on Team 47 members for the processes they had developed and the success of those processes for various areas of their work. Xerox called this team "The best of the best." The X-Team Award can be awarded to service, sales, management, or cross-functional teams. A maximum of three such awards may be granted each year.

Team 47 developed and documented processes to address most of the systems for which team members were responsible. This included systems at the team level, such as feedback and recognition, customer satisfaction, and integration of a new team member. The team also developed and documented systems at the organization level, such as parts tracking, machine maintenance, and retrofitting. To even be considered for the X-Team Award requires a rigorous interview and examination of work processes by a panel of corporate officers. Team 47 was the first service team to win this award in the history of Xerox. This team is now considered a benchmark within its organization.

It hasn't always been this way. In 1995, this high-volume and printing systems service team reached a low point in performance. Team members were frustrated with their manager, their performance, their merit increases, and even themselves. Merit increases were low because performance was mediocre. In fact, performance measures revealed that the team was performing at only minimally acceptable levels, which is a common characteristic of work groups that don't yet know how to take advantage of being a team. Sound familiar? Team members know how to do their own jobs as individuals, and they will continue to operate this way until something forces them to change. When Team 47's Employee Motivation and Satisfaction survey results came back at a meager 48 percent, that necessary force was unleashed. Team members affirmed their frustrations and dissatisfaction with each other and then asked themselves a critical question: "What are we going to do about this?" It was at this point that their self-awareness began. By asking this question, the team members realized they were an active agent in the mix and they empowered themselves to change their situation. This was the turning point for them as a team.

After their previous frustration, they became determined to become the best in their geographic region. Now that they had the desire, they needed the skills to operate as a team. Fortunately, there were several important resources Xerox could offer in support. First, there was a lot of information available from Xerox product and account tracking systems that were already in place. Second, it was standard policy for technicians to be trained to service multiple products. Finally, Xerox offered team-development support by making available previously developed processes for improvement and problem solving: the Nine-Step Quality Improvement Process and the Six-Step Problem Solving Process. (Both of these processes are discussed in further detail later in this chapter.) Although these resources had been available for a long time, it was only because Team 47 was now ready to take the next step in team development that they became meaningful.

Barriers to Change

Even with the desire to develop as a team and improve performance—and the useful resources Xerox had to offer—there were still tough challenges ahead. These individuals were new to the idea of working together as a team—only one had been part of the original Team 47, and none had any long-term experience of working in a group that functioned as a team in more than name only. To stop operating as individuals and begin to operate as a team, they would have to approach their workloads together, as a team. Thus they decided that no one would go home until everyone's work was finished each day. Given their circumstances, however, they were faced with some serious trust issues. They took

a leap of faith together that everyone would reciprocate commitment to the team-workload approach.

The other major hurdle was management. Before team members become high-performers, they usually do not have the skills to
manage themselves. The time when members begin to grow in
their ability to self-manage but are still not yet high-performers can
often be a frustrating period of growth for both managers and team
members. A manager doesn't want to give too much responsibility
without feeling confident that the team is capable of handling it. If
the team doesn't perform up to standards, it will be the manager
who is held accountable. At the same time, the team is groping for
more room to self-manage, but members are still on shaky ground
with new responsibilities and roles. It can be intimidating to take on
this responsibility without the confidence and insight that come
only with experience. Members of Team 47 accepted the challenge
of convincing their manager to give them the room to learn how
to be a team. The Employee Motivation and Satisfaction survey
results presented the needed forum to negotiate for that room.
Whenever substandard results occur at Xerox, team managers or
supervisors are required to create an action plan in cooperation
with the team to remedy the problem. The members of Team 47
told their manager that if he would give them the power, responsibility, and growing room to self-manage their team, he would never
see those kind of results again. The team manager closely monitored the team's performance through the Xerox product and
account tracking systems on a monthly basis. He agreed that so
long as performance remained at acceptable levels and improved
over time, he would continue to allow the team to self-manage.
They now had the freedom to go to school on becoming a team.

Measurement and Processes

Xerox has determined its own vital measures of performance. This
provides the structure for Xerox's Performance Report Card measurement system. The Performance Report Card is a percent-of-

goal-accomplished type of measurement system. This type of system has the option of creating a composite score, but Team 47 works quite effectively without one.

The dimensions of performance incorporated into Xerox's performance measures address common areas of interest to most businesses: reliability, customer satisfaction, efficiency with resources, timely product delivery. Table 5.1 presents the dimensions and measures for service teams at Xerox.

Reliability is measured specifically by the amount of ongoing maintenance that is required per million copies on machines. Customer service is measured through a follow-up survey conducted by Xerox operators. Efficiency of resources is measured in several ways through the parts budget. If teams are performing high-quality service on machines, replacement parts will be needed less frequently, thus reducing customer costs in service and parts. Teams are given a budget with which to buy parts, within the Xerox infrastructure, for the products they service. Maintaining reasonable budget levels per month measures efficiency of this resource. When parts are not used, there is a three-week deadline for unused parts to be returned to the depot. This is also a measure of resource efficiency. Finally, timely product delivery is measured by meeting the customer's requested servicing time. This is actually a procedure that Team 47 created and was later implemented company-wide due to

Table 5.1   Team Performance Measures

Dimensions	Measures
Customer satisfaction	Post service call survey
Reliability	Ongoing maintenance per million copies
Timeliness	Meeting customer-determined service time
Budgeting resources	Parts
Budgeting resources	Parts overdue

Source: Xerox Corporation. Used by permission.

its tremendous success and positive customer response. When a service request is called in, the customer determines on a scale of one to three how urgently servicing is needed. If it isn't urgent, team members have the flexibility to schedule service within the week at their convenience. If it is urgent, team members respond within two hours. This is where being a team can really pay off. Sometimes the particular team member who is responsible for the urgent account already has a full workload for the day and cannot respond within two hours. This team member can call in for another team member who is skilled in servicing the same product line to help cover the immediate work overload. While this is a noble idea in theory, many groups can recognize that this is a level of commitment to your team members that would not be easily attained. Doing someone else's work for them is a pretty big favor, but after being on the receiving end a few times, members of Team 47 are unwaveringly committed to approaching their workloads as a team in this manner. Table 5.2 shows Team 47's scores on these measures at the end of 1998. On every measure, Team 47 clearly outperforms the standards.

Teams have slightly more control when it comes to setting goals. During an annual review of performance for each team, members can adjust team targets in cooperation with their managers. As performance improves, teams are given more leeway in

Table 5.2   Team Score Card

Measures	1998 Standards	1998 Year-End Scores
Post service call survey (percent)	94.7	100
Ongoing maintenance per million copies (percent)	100	141.1
Customer-determined service time (percent)	70	107.8
Parts (percent of plan)	100	125
Parts overdue	$250	$76

Source: Xerox Corporation. Used by permission.

setting their own goals. Team pride and the value of challenging goals motivate members of Team 47 to set their goals a little higher than their district's goals every year. It is this competitiveness and drive for higher performance that makes Team 47 approach self-management like a mini-business within the organization.

Feedback is probably the most important aspect of Team 47's high performance. Generally, each team member is responsible for one dimension (parts, customer service, reliability, and so on) and reporting on it during each team meeting. So far, this may sound like any typical team meeting, but it is specifically how the team members give feedback to each other and what they do with that feedback that sets them apart from typical teams. The data available from Xerox's product and account tracking systems offers a great deal of information on day-to-day operations of each team. Most of this information is compiled into the specific measures on the team's report card, and the rest of the information supplements these measures. This supplemental information can be used to enhance problem solving by revealing performance problems that may not be obvious in the report card measures alone.

Xerox has recently begun to make this information available on an internal Web site, accessible to all employees. Before each team meeting, members gather information from this Web site regarding their team's performance for the month. Other teams' performance may also be gathered through this Web site for comparison. Previously, there was a two-month lag between the time of actual performance and the date that a team would receive feedback on that performance. Currently, the Web site information is one month old, a big improvement but still far from ideal. Xerox's goal is to post the information within five days of performance. During meetings, each member reports not only the score for each measure but other supplemental information as well. For example, a general reliability score is reported, but reliabilities may be discussed on each specific product line serviced by the team in order to look for a particular area of weakness that is bringing down the overall reliability score. By going into more detail than is outlined by the measures on the report card, the team is identifying smaller components that affect each measure. This makes problem solving and paths to improvement more recognizable and manageable.

If any measure reveals substandard performance, the team initiates the Six-Step Problem Solving Process presented in Figure 5.1. The Six-Step is a problem-solving mechanism that Xerox has trained all team members to use. It encompasses six tasks to help facilitate problem solving that could be applied to any kind of problem. Each step also identifies the type of outcome that should result from completing the tasks. If evaluation of the solution in Step 6 determines that the solution is not satisfactory, the process is recycled or repeated, beginning again at Step 1.

The pay-for-performance incentive program at Xerox underwent considerable changes for 1999. Previously, incentive bonuses were based on percentages of each goal that were met at year-end. One hundred points were divided across all the measures, similar to assigning importance weights to each dimension under the ProMES for Teams approach discussed in Chapter Four. In theory, if only 80 percent of a year-end goal was achieved, then only 80 percent of the incentive points possible for that measure were awarded. However, this was not the case. An 80 percent goal attainment was not considered "high performance" warranting incentive pay. So the team had to exceed the 80 percent level of goal attainment to get any incentive. Furthermore, 100 percent of the incentive points for a given measure were awarded only when a goal was significantly overachieved. The percentage of incentive points awarded out of a possible 100 was used to determine bonuses. Thus, if only 85 incentive points were awarded, then every member of the team received 85 percent of the maximum $1,000 per team member bonus. Last year, Team 47 achieved over 100 percent of all year-end goals, and, therefore, every team member was awarded the maximum of $1,000.

The new incentive program is a bit more complex. Before even being eligible to participate in the incentive program, a team must be certified in the first of two certification phases. Phase One

Figure 5.1   Six-Step Problem Solving Process

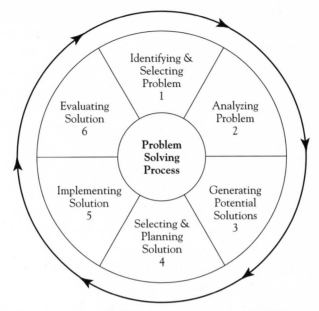

1 TASKS
- Identify problem topic
- Examine data about extent/nature of problem and relationship to business objectives
- Use data to describe "as is" and "desired state" of problem

OUTCOME
- Problem statement written in terms of gap between "as is" and "desired state"

2 TASKS
- List possible causes
- Identify probable causes
- Identify/prioritize root causes

OUTCOME
- Selected root causes to work on
- Revised problem statement if required

3 TASKS
- Review problem statement and root causes
- Generate list of potential solutions
- Clarify potential solutions

OUTCOME
- Produce list of as many ways as possible to solve problem

4 TASKS
- Determine selection criteria
- Select/agree on solution(s) to implement
- Develop plan to implement solution
- Develop plan to monitor/evaluate solution, including measures

OUTCOME
- Decide on optimum solution and plan its implementation

5 TASKS
- Follow implementation plan
- Use tracking system established in Step 4 to monitor/evaluate progress/effectiveness of solution
- Implement contingency plans as required

OUTCOME
- Group members/others implementing and monitoring solution

6 TASKS
- Compile/display collected data
- Compare with Step 1 business objectives/ "desired state"
- Compare with Step 2 "current state"
- Check for new problems created by solution
- Recycle through process to address additional problem/causes as needed

OUTCOME
- Group learns how effectively solution solved the identified problem

Source: Xerox Corporation. Used by permission.

Certification is achieved by developing and documenting all processes involved in a team's work, then subsequently having those processes approved by the team manager. Approval of a team's processes by upper management is required to attain Phase Two Certification. Teams must reach certain performance goals or targets each quarter on reliability, parts, and customer satisfaction. Xerox determined these three areas to be the most critical to a team's performance. Team managers and team members set the goals together on each measure. One point is awarded per measure every quarter if the goal is met. If all three targets are met in a quarter, then an additional point is awarded for a possible total of 4 points per quarter and 16 points per year. A one-time-only extra point is awarded for Phase Two Certification. At the end of the year, the points accrued by all teams in the state are added up and divided into $3,000 to determine the dollar value per point. The dollar value per point is then multiplied by a given team's total points for the year to determine the bonus for each team member. For example, if all teams in the state of Arkansas accumulated a total of 125 points for the year, then the dollar value per point would be $24 ($3,000 / 125). Thus, if a team achieved 16 total points for the year, then each member of that team would receive a bonus of $384 ($24 * 16).

The teams don't interact with each other in any way that would allow members of one team to undercut the performance of another, so there's no way to work the system so as to reduce the overall number of points used in computing the bonus value. The only way to increase a team's bonus is to get as many points as possible for that team.

Even though the possible bonus amount of this system has been significantly stepped down from a more lucrative incentive level, team pride drives members of Team 47 to maintain a strong commitment to continuous high performance. Members of Team 47 generally try to set their goals just above those of every other team in their region. They are not trying to compete with their peers but rather to compete with their own best performance. They have team pride in being high performers and simply want to continue to be the best.

As mentioned earlier, Team 47 received the X-Team Award for the processes the team had developed and the success of those processes for various areas of the team's work. The Nine-Step Quality Improvement Process, presented in Figure 5.2, was offered to all teams in Xerox training and was a key tool in developing processes to address various areas of work. Team members set about creating a process for nearly every aspect of their work that would benefit from having a formal approach. Once developed, these documented outlines offered a step-by-step process by which to carry out a specified task or aspect of work. The team member who created a particular process was named the process owner.

The Nine-Step Process is presented in a flow chart; subsequent processes developed with this method also use the flow chart format. There are three phases: planning for quality, organizing for quality, and monitoring for quality. Each step within the phase has a specific, single-minded target to be answered or identified. Answering or identifying each target in the flow chart walks you through a process step by step. For instance, the first step is to identify what the output of the process should be. Next, identify the customer and the customer's needs or requirements. Those requirements are then translated into specifications that are in terms of the work that a team performs. These targets or tasks make up the planning for quality phase. The organizing for quality phase identifies steps in the work process, selects measurements, and determines the ability level for producing the output by following the team process. If this last step cannot be attained, the team engages in problem solving. The last phase, monitoring for quality, encompasses actual production of output, evaluating output, and determining if the product is satisfactory or not. If the product is found to be unsatisfactory, the process is recycled, using the information from the first round to develop a better approach.

Here are some examples of processes that Team 47 developed: meeting customer-requested response times, planning to cover

Figure 5.2 Nine-Step Quality Improvement Process

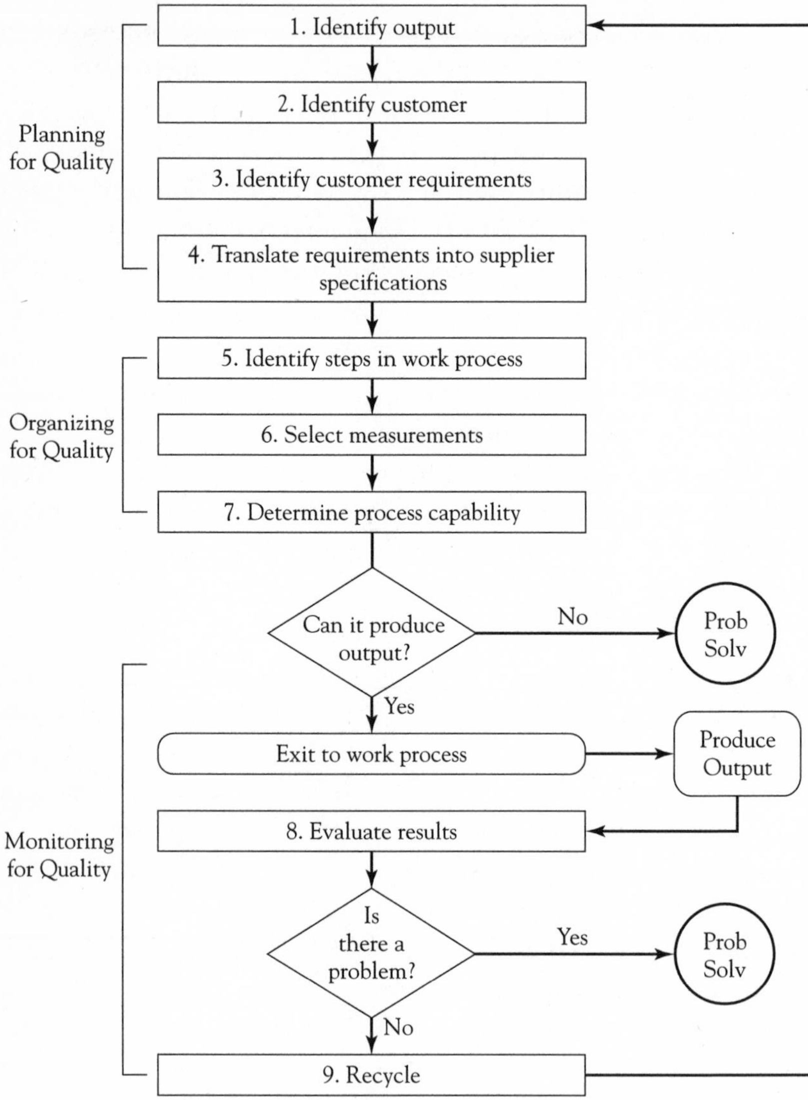

Source: Xerox Corporation. Used by permission.

absences of team members for vacation or training, integrating new team members, planning overtime, giving recognition and feedback, conducting team meetings, returning parts, and taking noncompliance or disciplinary action for a team member who does not follow established team processes. Team 47 also used the Nine-Step Process to outline expectations and norms concerning things such as time management, backing up team members with their work, following established processes, professionalism, parts management, overtime, and quality of maintenance. One critical trait of members in Team 47, again similar to business partners, is that they are constantly using their measures and processes to find ways to avoid problems that may arise in the future. Members don't wait until there is a crisis and then react. If performance levels aren't where team members expect them to be, the processes are reworked and reevaluated to see if a better process might prevent the problem. As with any businesses, to thrive they must use a proactive approach to their performance in the marketplace.

Part of the organizational support offered by Xerox is cross-training for most or all team members. In the case of Team 47, the combined skills of all members span twenty-four product lines. It may not be feasible to have every member cross-trained to service all twenty-four product lines, but there is a great deal of overlap in product line skills across members. This allows team members the flexibility to be highly committed to the balancing of their work-loads as a team. This balancing of the team workload has posi-tively affected several areas. It has helped maintain quick or on-time responses to customer calls, which in turn has contributed to good customer service and relations. With good relations, customers have typically been more flexible, when possible, with the requested response times for their service. This has allowed the team considerably more flexibility to meet customers' needs and still assist each other when there are overloads on individual workloads.

Results

As the team's performance has improved overall, the quality of service to the customers has inherently improved also. Customers have received more consideration by being allowed to determine the time frame within which they will receive service. Team members take pride in their work and are greatly motivated to continue their high performance. In meetings, all members show a strong discipline for applying the processes that have helped them become high performers. In fact, these processes have become a fluid part of the language or terminology they use to communicate with each other. Members stay focused and invested in the discussion throughout meetings. They have a deep sense of ownership in their work, and they simply "believe in what they are doing." Figure 5.3 presents Team 47's scores on customer service between 1996 and 1998. The overall trend of improvement in their scores is clearly visible.

The best teams operate as business partners rather than as employees. Team 47 made the transition to business partnership after a low point in its performance. Team members' attitudes, ownership mentality, quality service, and customer consideration nourished the rapport between the team and its customers. This is the

Figure 5.3   Customer Service Satisfaction

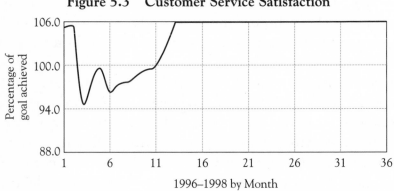

1996–1998 by Month

Source: Xerox Corporation. Used by permission.

very kind of relationship that organizations seek to establish with customers because this type of relationship keeps them happy and coming back for more. In a large corporation, this is possible only if team members operate as an extension of the organization's philosophies and strategies—that is, as business partners.

Assessing Your Team

1. Low scores on the performance measures galvanize some teams into action, while others become defensive and reduce their commitment to the work. What makes the difference?

2. What is required for teams to engage in productive problem solving and process improvement?

3. Managers are often accused of being afraid of releasing control. What do managers need in order to give their teams more autonomy in decision making and in managing their own performance?

4. What is the difference between team members as employees and team members as business partners? How are the team meetings different?

5. What role do performance measures play in teams that function as business partners?

Team 47 is a service team at Xerox Corporation. Team members can be reached at the following address: Xerox Corporation, c/o Team 47, 10801 Executive Center Drive, Shannon Building, Suite 100, Little Rock, AR 72211.

Tressa Cherry is a graduate student in industrial and organizational psychology at Middle Tennessee State University.

Chapter Six

Measurement in a Continuous Process Environment

Eastman Chemical Company

By Mark Cappellino

Performance measurement can use numerical data provided on a regular basis or it can use nonnumeric information such as a checklist. Either way, successful measurement requires a disciplined approach. Discipline in this context is the result of a meaningful and user-friendly system that engenders follow-through and ownership. This case study presents the successful efforts of one manufacturing operation at Eastman Chemical Company that combined the simple notion of proactive measurement with ownership and specific team focus to gain great advantage in achieving a strategic objective.

Continuous process manufacturing operations typically have problems resulting from differences across work shifts. In the case of the Cellulosics Manufacturing Operation (CMO) at Eastman Chemical Company, the amount of process variability between multiple shifts resulted in variability in product color, consistency, and reliability. The leaders of this group made it their strategic intent to reduce this process variability; they developed a team-driven measurement system to pursue this goal. The basic approach to the Integrated Process Management (IPM) system is to develop standardized operating procedures to respond to input variability across shifts. Maintaining consistent procedures for adjusting machine feed rates in response to variability in raw material is an example of what CMO managers wanted to accomplish.

Eastman Chemical Company is a 1993 winner of the Malcolm Baldrige National Quality Award. The CMO produces specialty raw materials in various forms, colors, and consistencies for use in plastic molding manufacturing.

CMO managers developed the IPM over the course of the year leading up to its implementation in March 1997. They spent that year going to team meetings throughout the operation introducing the IPM system. They visited all teams from safety and engineering to manufacturing and production control. Information was shared about which specific process controls would be targeted, the numbering system that would be used, and the format and paperwork that would be required to support the IPM. It was in these meetings that management discussed with teams and team managers the importance of their involvement in order to realize successful implementation of the IPM system. The individuals who would participate on the IPM team were selected from these team meetings based on expressed interest and process knowledge. Once team members were identified, management and team members participated in four eight-hour training sessions that took place off-site.

Today the IPM team, comprising roughly fifteen people from all areas of the operation, meets every morning. They subscribe to a measurement discipline that is driven by the process of completing the shift checklists and using an overhead projector to present them in the meeting. While this form of measurement is less formal and cumbersome than a strict quantitative approach, it has proven to be very effective at monitoring the relatively stable processes within CMO. The checklists are working documents that are not only a record of information, they are integral to actual process control. The fact that everyone must fill out the checklists adds to the standardization of the process. The checklist format provides an added personal benefit to its users by engendering follow-through and ownership. Every IPM team member is responsible for reporting some information or data by way of the checklists in the morning meetings. Presenting information to the group—and knowing that the whole operation is going to rely on that information—reinforces each team member's sense of ownership and pride. When IPM team members put their initials on a checklist (see Exhibit 6.1), they are holding themselves accountable to the entire operation. One person records all this information on a computer terminal as it is presented and sends it to all members of the organization over the intranet after each daily meeting.

Employees from all areas of the operation have real-time access to this information from computer terminals throughout the facility. They rely on this information for feedback on the preceding day's performance and to make decisions about the coming day's production activity. For example, employees may make decisions on the manufacturing floor to change production schedules, machine feed rates, or maintenance schedules. Those responsible for production scheduling and inventory control may make decisions about raw material purchase levels or which products to run on which machines and for how long. All of these decisions are guided by the standards that all employees have developed through the IPM system. The standards that guide all aspects of the operation are in turn maintained and monitored by the IPM team.

This feedback loop and continual monitoring of information reinforces both accountability and ownership of results among all employees. The heart of the success of the IPM system rests in the employees' pride in solving problems as they arise. The system empowers employees to identify and control key variables and—most important—it reinforces their behavior on a daily basis by way of the checklist and daily meeting feedback. It was noted by one IPM team member that on one day when the intranet was down, team members in the plant had an immediate reaction to the void of information and were concerned about how they were doing. They have grown dependent on this feedback as a tool for planning and monitoring their work. The system holds them accountable for achieving production goals while maintaining continuity between shifts. The IPM system has fostered a sense of business partnership among the employees of the Cellulosics Manufacturing Operation.

Exhibit 6.1   CMO Process Control Checklist

Twin-screw extruder checklist

Unit No._____   Date_____   Crew_____   Days   Nights

1. Extruder
   A. B. C. D.

   A. Check feed system set-up
   B. Check set-up conditions
   C. Visually inspect manual PZ and stabilizer valves
   D. Check for revised batch card and packaging instructions
   E. Check all twi's and sign new ones
   F. Print order schedule at start of shift and at order change
   G. Check scales on weekends and holidays
   H. Complete the fork lift inspection sheet (day shift only)

2.	Prod. Lot No.	Formula	Clean up Min.	Type Count.	Initials
A.	_____	_____	_____	_____	_____
B.	_____	_____	_____	_____	_____
C.	_____	_____	_____	_____	_____
D.	_____	_____	_____	_____	_____

3.   Downtime: Min.
      _____   _____
      _____   _____
      _____   _____
      _____   _____

      Corrective Action:
      _____   _____
      _____   _____
      _____   _____
      _____   _____

4.   Deviation from process standard: (Comment at bottom of page)
          Standard No.   Order No.

          _____   _____
          _____   _____
          _____   _____

5.   Housekeeping
      Y N
          A. Haul off empty drums and trash
          B. All non-conforming material labeled and disposed of properly
          C. Floor free of dirt
          D. Was process and housekeeping satisfactory from previous shift? If not,
             please comment below
      Comments: (Over if necessary)
      _____
      _____
      _____
      _____

      _____

                          Operator's Signature _____

Source: Eastman Chemical Company. Used by permission.

Before the implementation of the IPM system in March 1997, information regarding critical process variables was maintained in logbooks, which is how it was communicated between shifts. Information was either misrecorded, recorded and misplaced, or in some cases just never recorded. There was a general air of disorganization and if any unacceptable product output was identified it would often be difficult to determine exactly what to change at the input end. There was little continuity between shifts therefore good product quality was left in large part to the chance of operating variances between individuals of different shifts. As a result, CMO was experiencing considerable variability with on-time delivery to their customers. For the year preceding implementation of the IPM, average on-time delivery percentage was 92.8 percent (See Figure 6.1).

CMO has realized many improvements with the IPM system. On-time delivery improved during the implementation of the

Figure 6.1   On-Time Delivery

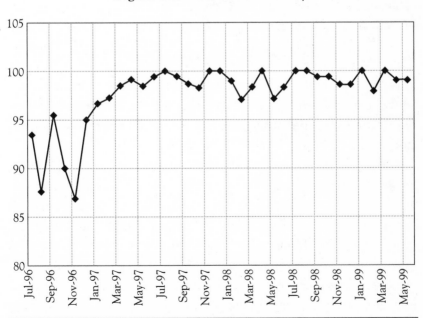

Source: Eastman Chemical Company. Used by permission.

system and stabilized at the higher level thereafter (as noted in Figure 6.1). In addition to improving delivery performance, the IPM system enabled increased productivity and greater efficiency in the manufacturing operation. The members of the IPM team indicated that they had increased production volume in spite of having to operate with a reduced workforce resulting from company-wide reorganization. Team members attribute that ability to operate more efficiently with a leaner staff to the fact that the IPM system has opened communication between shifts, making shift changes virtually seamless. Employees are able to anticipate production control problems and solve them proactively because of increased scheduling visibility. The daily meetings have become essentially informal problem-solving and problem-avoidance meetings, eliminating the disruptions that were once a direct result of the shifts' operating in a vacuum with respect to one another.

Another benefit of the IPM system that all members seemed to echo is the improved relationships between management and manufacturing employees. One operator said that he had never seen communication so good between management and the employees. It can only be assumed that the increased accountability and autonomy from the employees' standpoint is welcome and supported by the management team that developed the IPM system. The IPM team members have solved a major problem for the operation and the measurement system reinforces that pride every day in the team meetings and with the operation-wide communication of information. The motivation to continually improve the operation is in turn driven by this continual feedback.

Mark Cappellino has fifteen years' experience in manufacturing, having held positions as project manager, assembly business unit manager, and VP of marketing and sales. He has helped organizations with transformations to TQM and lean manufacturing. He has formal education in engineering and industrial and organizational psychology, with three years of experience with team problem-solving training, measurement and incentives, and general management training. Mark is a partner in the Alignment Group.

Chapter Seven

Automating Measurement

Customizing the Accompanying Spreadsheet

Two team members are talking:

> *Joel:* This new measurement system we're getting, I'm afraid it's just going to be a lot of work for us to keep up with the data.
>
> *Liz:* I think we should be able to understand the system ourselves, rather than waiting on the central office to produce the reports for us. I want to verify the incentive calculations for our team.

A good measurement system should streamline a team's work. By bringing together the key performance measures and focusing the team on those measures through problem solving, the measurement system should help the team concentrate its energies. The team should focus its energies on solving key business problems. The team should not be burdened with distracting information, yet it needs detailed performance data regarding problems it is solving.

Many teams want to keep track of their own performance measurement data. This helps the team members further understand their measurement system and check the accuracy of the data. When they say, "We want to be trained to track our own performance measures," that is a good sign. It means they want ownership.

Software to Automate the Measurement System

To automate the measurement system, a spreadsheet or a database that contains the performance data can be used to track data over time. There are several avenues for implementing this.

Commercially available software programs specifically designed for team performance measurement are discussed at the end of this chapter. These programs will create a spreadsheet or database specifically designed for a team's needs, after a series of question-and-answer specifications are completed. These programs can be costly, but you probably already have a spreadsheet program capable of readily handling the data and graphics required for a team measurement system. With some work, a program such as Excel can produce an excellent format for computerizing the measurement of a team's performance.

Using the File That Accompanies This Book

Included with this book is a generic spreadsheet for a team performance measurement system. The spreadsheet is on the accompanying CD-ROM under the filename "Generic.xls." This is an Excel file for Office 97. The file does not have a copyright imprint, and the rights to use and copy the file are included in the purchase price of this book. Use of this file will be explained as you work through this chapter. Use of the spreadsheet assumes completion of the activities at the end of Chapters One through Four. Decisions made in these activities will determine inputs for the spreadsheet.

By working through this chapter, you may customize the accompanying spreadsheet to fit your team. To begin, copy the file "Generic.xls" to your computer. Start Excel (Office 97 or more recent version) and open the file "Generic.xls." If asked about macros, click on "enable."

Entering the Dimensions and Measures

Click on the tab of the spreadsheet named "My Team." This is where you will enter the dimensions and measures from the activities at the end of Chapter Two. In Column A, enter the dimension names in the appropriate cells, beginning in cell A4. If you have more than five dimensions, you will need to insert at least three new rows for each additional dimension. Inserting rows gives you blank, unformatted lines. Once you've added the number of rows you need, copy the corresponding rows from an existing dimension into them to pick up the formatting, then enter the dimension names in the appropriate cells. You can update the rest of the cells later. (For everything you add, you will need to make adjustments to the instructions in this chapter that refer to specific rows. For instance, if you add one dimension with one measure, then when the instructions tell you to do something at row 60, you will need to go to row 63.)

After the dimensions have been entered, enter the names of the measures in column A under their corresponding dimension. If you have more than one measure per dimension, you will need to add two rows for each additional measure, using the insert command. (Keep track of the number of rows you add for dimensions and measures, and adjust the instructions for subsequent sections of the spreadsheet accordingly.) Included in the workbook is an example from the Square D assembly team discussed in Chapter Two. Click on the tab for the sheet named "Example 1" and take a look at column A. Your spreadsheet should resemble Figure 7.1. If you have more than one measure per dimension, look at "Example 2." Your spreadsheet should resemble Figure 7.2. For now, only focus on column A; the other columns will be addressed later. If your team chooses not to have a composite score, you can skip ahead to the section on graphing.

General Forms of the Measures

The file "Generic.xls" already contains the necessary formulas to create the composite score. However, the formulas may not be in the proper places for the specific measurement system you are creating. The next decision concerns the general form of each measure. A measure such as productivity, where a larger number means better performance, is called an *increasing* form. Conversely, a measure such as defects per unit, where a larger number means worse performance, is a *diminishing* form. Before going any further, make

Figure 7.1   Example of One Measure Per Dimension

Quality
Defects per unit
Productivity
Book$ per labor hour
On-time shipments
Percent jobs finished on schedule
Cycle time
Average cycle time in days
Assembly start
Percent of jobs ready to start on time

Figure 7.2   Example of More Than One Measure Per Dimension

Quality
Defects per unit
Customer Satisfaction Survey
Productivity
Book$ per labor hour
On time
Percent jobs finished on schedule
Cycle time
Average cycle time in days
Assembly start
Percent of jobs ready to start on time

a note on a piece of paper as to which form each of your measures takes.

Now you will copy the appropriate form to each measure. Begin with your first measure; if it is an increasing form, it is correct the way it is. If it is a diminishing form, it should be changed. Let's assume that it is a diminishing form, as defects per unit is in "Example 1," so you can learn how to change it. Go to the sheet named "Example 1." You will copy a diminishing form on to the increasing form that is currently in place for defects per unit. Begin by highlighting the cells for the nearest diminishing form: cells C8 to I9. Copy these cells to the Clipboard in Excel (that is, highlight them and then press Ctrl-C), and then place the insertion point on cell C5 and execute the paste command (Ctrl-V). This procedure copies the proper diminishing form cells to the defects per unit measure. In "Example 1" your spreadsheet should now have a diminishing form for rows 5 and 6. Compare these rows on your sheet "Example 1" to the sheet "Example 1 (2)," which has been corrected. Your two rows for the measure of defects per unit should resemble Figure 7.3.

If any change is necessary to the form of your first measure in the sheet "My Team," make that change now. After making the changes, your sheet named "My Team" should have the proper form on rows 5 and 6. Check with the notes you made earlier on the form for each measure to make sure this is correct.

Experience has shown that this procedure for correcting the forms requires special attention. With this in mind, the exercise will repeat the steps with another example, just to ensure that your understanding is complete. Go back to the sheet "Example 1" and move down to the productivity measure of Book$ per labor hour. This measure should have an increasing form, but it currently has a diminishing form. To make the correction, copy the nearest increasing form measure: Percent jobs finished on schedule. Highlight cells C11 through I12 and copy them to the Clipboard. Move to cell C8, and execute the paste command. Now you should have an increasing form for the productivity measure. Your rows 8 and 9 should resemble the corresponding rows in "Example 1 (2)." The first two measures in the sheet "Example 1" should now resemble

Figure 7.3   Example of a Correct General Form

September	Data	Effectiveness	Goal	General Form	Top 1/2	Beyond
Quality						
# Defects per unit	0.10	35.00		Diminishing	35	35
				Diminishing		35

Figure 7.4. (Note: If you have any cells that say "#NAME?," ignore them for now.)

Make any necessary changes to the forms for the rest of the measures in your sheet "My Team." Each form for each measure should now match the notes you made earlier.

Importance Weights

Using the importance weights developed in Chapter Four, Table 4.5, you will further customize the spreadsheet. Go to the sheet "My Team" and put in a short name in column J (so it doesn't exceed the width of the column) for each of the measures; this will make it easier to see where the importance weights should go. Now put the importance weights for the measures in column K on the rows for the appropriate measures. The importance weight for your first measure should go in cell K5, the weight for the second measure should go in cell K8, and so on. The sum of the importance weights in column K should equal 100—double-check this, as the spreadsheet won't give you an error message if they don't. Your sheet "My Team" should now resemble columns J and K in the sheet "Example 1 (2)," except you should have different measures and different weights. Figure 7.5 presents an example of how these two columns should appear. You may still have some cells that say "#NAME?" in columns C, H, or I; ignore them for now.

Figure 7.4 Example of Correct General Forms for Two Measures

September	Data	Effectiveness	Goal	General Form	Top 1/2	Beyond
Quality						
# Defects per unit	0.10	35.00		Diminishing	35	35
				Diminishing		35
Productivity						
Book$ per labor	$ 300	3.33		Increasing	3.33333	#NAME?
hour				Increasing		#NAME?

Figure 7.5   Example of Importance Weights
for Measures

Measure	Weight percent of 100
Defects	35
Book$	10
On time	25
Cycle time	15
Assem. St.	15

Performance Standards

The next step relies on Table 4.6 from the end of Chapter Four. In the sheet "My Team," insert the best case values in column L from Table 4.6. Insert the worst case values in column M, and insert the minimally acceptable values in column N. Your sheet "My Team" should now resemble the sheet "Example 1 (2)" shown in Figure 7.6, except that your values will be different. Carefully check the three values for each of the performance standards. This is the place where mistakes are most often made in customizing the worksheet. For example, putting a worst case value in the row for the best case value will invalidate your formula. You still may have some cells that say "#NAME?," in columns C, H, or I; those will be taken care of next.

Formatting Cells

The cells that hold the data and the performance standards may need to be formatted differently from what they are now. Go to sheet "Example 1," and go to the productivity measure, Book$ per labor hour. This measure should have a dollar format. Highlight cell B8, and format the cell in dollars by clicking the dollar symbol on the toolbar at the top of the screen. Do the same for the performance standards in cells L8, M8, and N8. If you also put in the best case of 350, worst case of 200, and minimally acceptable of 275, row 8 in "Example 1" should resemble row 8 in the finished

Figure 7.6   Example of Performance Standards

Performance Standards

Best Case 0.15	Worst Case 0.5	Minimal Acceptable 0.3
Best Case $ 350	Worst Case $ 200	Minimal Acceptable $ 275
Best Case 95 percent	Worst Case 60 percent	Minimal Acceptable 80 percent
Best Case 10	Worst Case 20	Minimal Acceptable 15
Best Case 85 percent	Worst Case 50 percent	Minimal Acceptable 65 percent

example in "Example 1 (2)," with each of the performance standards displayed in dollars. If you type in 300 in the data cell (B8), it should be displayed in dollar format. Cell C8 should be displayed as 3.33; this shows that the formula is working correctly. If more (or fewer) decimals appear than you want, you can change these by highlighting the appropriate cells and then clicking the decimal increase or decrease buttons on the toolbar.

In a similar fashion, you can format cells in percent format. Go back to the sheet "Example 1" and highlight cell B11. This cell needs to be in percent format, so click on the percent button on the toolbar. Do the same for cells L11, M11, and N11. Now, type in the best case of 0.95, worst case of 0.60, and minimally acceptable of 0.80 in row 11. (Note that if you enter 95 instead of 0.95, the cell may display 9500%—this happens in some versions of Excel, while others will give you 95% for either entry.) Next, enter the value 0.85 in the data cell B11. Your version of the worksheet "Example 1" should resemble row 11 in the worksheet "Example 1

(2)" showing an effectiveness score of 8.33. Return to your team's worksheet ("My Team") and make any necessary formatting changes so that the formatting is consistent with the type of measures you have.

Creating a Feedback Report with Current Data

The spreadsheet needs data in order to produce a feedback report. If no current data exists, you may use your best estimate of the team's current performance. However, data is needed for each of the measures. Enter the current performance data into column B in the sheet "My Team."

You will notice that the effectiveness scores in column C change as you input the current data. Your sheet should resemble Figure 7.7, allowing for the fact that you have different measures and data. Once you have entered the data for all your measures, you should no longer see cells that display "#NAME?" in column C. If you do, there is a problem, probably in the cell formatting or in

Figure 7.7   Example Feedback Report

Team Performance

September	*Data*	*Effectiveness*
Quality		
# Defects per unit	0.10	35.00
Productivity		
Book$ per labor hour	$ 300	3.33
On-time shipments		
Percent jobs finished on schedule	85 percent	8.33
Cycle time		
Average cycle time in days	9.00	15.00
Assembly start		
Percent of jobs ready to start on time	90 percent	15.00
Group Performance Index		76.67

the form (increasing or diminishing) of the measures. There may be some cells in column H or I that display "#NAME?"; this is OK. It just means that your data is outside the range of those formulas.

Find the composite score at the bottom of column C; it is called the group performance index or GPI. (Feel free to rename it.) This composite number should be between –100 and +100, and it is a percent. In the sheet "Example 1 (2)," the GPI is 76.67, indicating that this team is at 76.67 percent of its best possible performance for that time period. If the team had an incentive system, it might get 76.67 percent of the possible bonus.

As a quality control check, compare the effectiveness values for each measure against what you should get from the contingency graphs you drew by hand for the last exercise in Chapter Four. To do this, find the current data on the horizontal axis of a figure, go up to the slanting line and across to the vertical axis. That score should roughly match the effectiveness score in column C. See Figure 7.8 for an example based on the productivity measure of Book$ per labor hour. Note that on the feedback report the team had a score of $300 on its productivity measure; that score translated to an effectiveness score of 3.3. This data roughly matches what we find on the graph. If the effectiveness scores do not roughly match, you may need to redraw the graph, using graph paper. After comparing the new drawing to the spreadsheet, if there are still inconsistencies, there is a problem in the spreadsheet—double-check the general form, the importance weight, and the performance standards.

If the general form is increasing, the numbers on the horizontal axis should get larger, moving from left to right. The opposite holds true for the diminishing form. The importance weights should correspond to the height of the vertical axis in your drawing. If a measure has an importance weight of 10, the vertical axis in the drawing should range from –10 to 10, as it does in Figure 7.8. The performance standards should correspond to your drawing, just as they do in Figure 7.8.

**Figure 7.8   Quality Control Check of the Feedback Report
Against the Graphs**

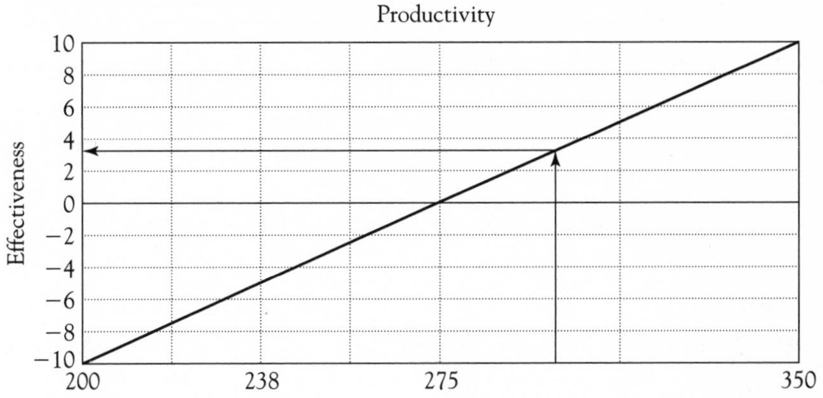

Productivity

Graphing

The preceding steps produce a feedback report with the team's current performance data. Based on the feedback report, the team can see how it is doing on each of its measures. However, for problem solving, the team will need the data displayed in graphs. Although there are many types of graphs the teams can use, the most common types are line graphs of performance trends over time, graphs of frequencies, and graphs of categories.

Graphs of Performance Trends. Most team members will want to see the composite score and the trends in their performance on each measure. This requires having data over time. You are now going to create some data and enter it in the graphing area. Begin by assuming that the current month is September. Click on the sheet "My Team" and enter September in cell A2. Then enter the monthly data—or whatever time period you choose for measurement. (Your measures don't all need to be on the same frequency. For instance, a team will often use both quarterly and monthly measures in the same system. In these cases, the team receives monthly feedback. It uses the same quarterly data each month, until the next quarter.) Begin in cell B60, and enter data in that column through August. For September, enter the GPI for the current month from the feedback sheet. Note that a line graph has formed in the lower right-hand graph named "GPI." Your graph for GPI should resemble that in Figure 7.9, except that your scores will be different.

Now you will graph the rest of your team's measures. Enter the names of your team's measures in row 58. That is, where it now says "Measure 1" in cell C58, enter a short name for that measure. Similarly, do the same for each of the measures. If you have more than five measures, just keep adding new names out to the right. The next step is to change the titles of each graph to match the names of the measures. To change the first graph title, click on the title of the graph now titled "Measure 1." Enter the name of your first measure, as per cell C58. Now, replace the rest of the graph titles with the names of your team's measures.

If you have added measures, you will have to add new graphs for them. Say you want to add a graph for one new measure. Put the name for your new measure in column H, just to the right of the name that used to be "Measure 5" (which you have probably changed to a meaningful name of your own by now). Then create a space for the new graph by inserting ten new rows beneath the graph that was titled "Measure 5."

Figure 7.9 Example Trend Graph for the Composite GPI Score

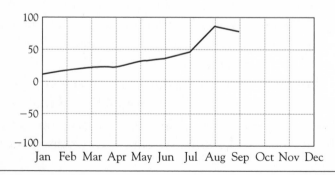

Next, click on the graph area for the graph that was titled "Measure 5." When you have clicked on the graph area, you should see six black handles (boxes) around the outside perimeter of the graph. Click on copy. Move the insertion point to the cell where you want the new graph to begin. Click on paste. A copy of the graph will appear. Drag the handles to resize it so that it is the same size as the other graphs. Next, change the source data so that it is calling on the data for the new measure in column H. Do this by clicking on the graph area of the new graph, then right-click, then choose source data, then series tab. You will now have to carefully edit the boxes that say "Name" and "Values." In both boxes, replace the reference to column G with a reference to the column for the new measure, column H. You should replace one G in the "Name" box and two G's in the "Values" boxes with H's. Then click OK, and the graph should read the monthly data you will enter for the new measure. The last change is to give the graph a meaningful title, just as you changed the titles of the other graphs.

To complete the trend graphs, enter historical data for each of your team's measures through August, beginning in cell C60. Next, enter the current data from the feedback sheet. Once this is finished, you should have line graphs for each measure that extend through September, like the one shown in Figure 7.10.

Figure 7.10   Example of a Trend Graph for One Measure

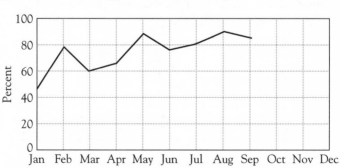

At this point, you have completed a feedback report and graphs for your team's measurement system. In the future, you can enter new data each month into both the feedback report and the graphs. You can also add text and data to the spreadsheet for long- and short-term goals in columns D, E, or F.

Graphs of Frequencies and Categories. To problem solve on a specific measure, the team will need to zoom in on that measure so as to determine what needs to be done to make improvements. This critical point directly connects the team performance measurement system to statistical process control and other TQM techniques. Therefore, for teams to implement a measurement system for problem solving, they must have knowledge of these techniques.

For example, examination of Figure 7.10 shows that this measure possesses a great deal of variability. It is always below the best-case standard of 95 percent for on-time shipments, so this measure presents a good opportunity for problem solving by the team. However, Figure 7.10 lacks the details needed for problem solving. For instance, the team may need to know how late the shipments are. A bar graph of the late items, indicating how late they are, can address that question. For instance, Figure 7.11 indicates that most of the items are only a day late.

Figure 7.11   Extent of "Lateness" of Shipped Items

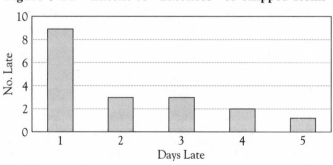

This graph indicates that the team may only need to make slight improvements, as opposed to a massive change. However, the graph does not tell the team where to focus its efforts. Figures 7.12 and 7.13 are category graphs that provide the kind of information the team needs to diagnose the problem and develop an action plan. Figure 7.12 indicates that most of the late shipments occur on Monday. So, the team may need to get most of the items due for Monday delivery finished on Friday. By examining the Pareto chart in Figure 7.13, the team may also see that most of the late shipments are Product C items. Therefore, the team may decide to institute a special procedure for these items.

These examples demonstrate that the team will need more details on measures that it wants to improve. Those details can be

Figure 7.12   Late Shipments by Day of Week

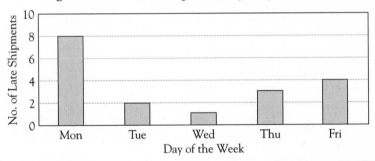

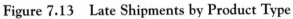

Figure 7.13   Late Shipments by Product Type

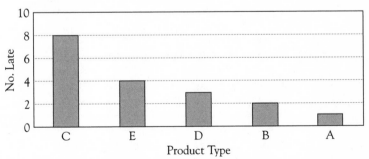

easily graphed, and they connect directly to TQM and statistical process control procedures.

Using the Percent-of-Goal Sheet

For those who prefer to use the percent-of-goal method to create the composite score, click on the worksheet titled "% of goal." The procedure for modifying this sheet is the same as for modifying the "My Team" sheet with a few changes. After personalizing the measures for your team, copying in the appropriate forms, and assigning importance weights as explained earlier in this chapter, there are three columns to complete.

First, fill in the column titled "Quarterly Goals" with the appropriate figures. While these numbers do not affect the calculations, they are important references for the team. Next fill in the column titled "Monthly Target." This column may be the same as the goal, but usually it is less ambitious, moving closer to the goal as the quarter progresses. The "Monthly Target" number will affect the calculation of the "Score" column. The team will have to achieve the target to get the highest possible score for a particular measure. Note that it can only score as high as the importance weight. Next, fill in the column titled "Threshold" (column K). This is the amount at which the incentive pay system would begin to apply. You can also think of it as the minimally acceptable value.

This completes the changes to the basic spreadsheet. You can follow the directions for changing the graphs from the preceding section.

Modifying the Spreadsheet to Accommodate Changes

Experience has shown that the measurement system needs to be revised about every year or two for most teams, or whenever they change processes, goals, or business strategy. The spreadsheet is designed to handle any changes your team might want to make to its measurement system. Simply replacing the old values with the new ones can change the importance weights and performance standards. Always do a quality control check to make sure the new values are correct. The importance weights should add to 100, and the performance standards should match a graph you would draw by hand. The measures can be changed, or new ones can be added, by following the steps at the beginning of this exercise.

Summary

Most teams will want to put their measurement system into a spreadsheet to make it easier to develop feedback reports. In fact, we find that usually there is at least one team member who is interested in taking over this task—it's a good way to expand personal skills, and it puts the team member at the center of the information network. This chapter provides detailed instructions for customizing the accompanying Excel workbook to fit the team's measurement system. There are templates for the ProMES for Teams method and the percent-of-goal method. By following the instructions, the team can take the measurement system it developed from the end-of-chapter exercises and put that system into a spreadsheet. The spreadsheet will then create the feedback report and make the appropriate graphs, which can be used for problem solving.

Chapter Eight

Performance Improvement Methods

Using Measurement to Spur Results

Two team members are talking:

> *Lindsay:* Now that we've finished developing our team scorecard,
> what are we supposed to do with it?
>
> *Sarah:* When we have meetings to go over our scorecard,
> everyone just sits there. The team leader makes all the
> decisions. The biggest decision we've made is where to have
> our team breakfast. I don't see why we even need teams if we
> never make any important decisions.

A Systems Model

Thus far this book has been about developing a system of measures that are in tune with an organization's strategy and meaningful to the accountable team members. But the measurement system is not an end in itself—on its own, it does little to advance the team's purpose. Measures simply provide a springboard for performance improvement. There must be a process for using measures to establish performance expectations, keep score against those expectations, and identify and remove barriers to achieving those expectations. Moreover, when noteworthy results are accomplished, reinforcement should be delivered to strengthen the responsible behaviors.

Conceptually, performance measures act as one of three lead systems that trigger and enable team improvement activities. Reinforcement, as the trailer system, makes it matter for team members to engage in these activities in ways that yield valuable performance gains. The improvement methodology employed by the team is the core system—the means by which team members solve problems and develop new ways of doing work. These systems are shown in Figure 8.1.

"We have teams, everyone has a scorecard and we've designed an incentive plan that can pay out as much as a 15 percent bonus each month; so why haven't the numbers improved?" a Fortune 25 division vice president once asked a consulting colleague of one of the authors. The consultant instantly replied, "The team problem-solving meetings have not led to any significant changes in the way work is done." This might seem to be a statement of the obvious, but it was nonetheless important. She was right. As the widely cited axiom goes, "If you do what you always did, you'll get what you always got." In this case, the prescription was evident: provide more training and support in problem solving and process management to the forty-five teams in the organization. But of course, this is not always the shortcoming.

The authors have devoted 80 percent of this book to the measurement system largely because our experience suggests it is often the root cause of failing improvement initiatives. As with the other lead systems, it is obviously crucial to get measurement off on the right foot or subsequent systems will suffer. The deficiency, more

Figure 8.1   Systems Model for Performance Improvement

Lead Systems	Core System	Trailer System
• Leadership • Training • Performance Measurement (*part of larger information system*)	• Team Problem Solving and Process Management (*performance improvement methods*)	• Reinforcement (*social recognition, incentives, and so on*)
Chapters 1–7	Chapter 8	Chapter 9

than with any other system, appears to be primarily due to a lack of knowledge and guidance. The main intent of the first seven chapters has been to rectify this. Nevertheless, the improvement story would be incomplete if the core and trailer systems were not addressed. They are equally vital, so this chapter will treat the performance improvement methods employed by teams and the next chapter will describe how improved performance can be effectively recognized.

Expanded Performance Improvement Cycle—PDAI

Often the method used to pursue performance improvement is based more on the latest fad than on what matches the teams' current needs. There are certainly numerous schools of thought, each with a box of tools and techniques, that are very attractive to those who may be desperately seeking answers to rather serious challenges. Total Quality Management (TQM), synchronous management (theory of constraints), value proposition and delivery, sociotechnical design, and process reengineering are perhaps the most popular paradigms of the past two or three decades. They all have something to offer and their concepts and tactics are not mutually exclusive—though if the purest disciples of these various schools were locked in a room and charged with solving a case study, there would probably be a few bumps and bruises before they ultimately announced they were at an impasse. Fortunately, converging principles and practices can be integrated into a cohesive improvement process.

Based on W. E. Deming's plan-do-check-act (PDCA) cycle and similar continuous improvement cycles, the following PDAI (plan-do-assess-improve) framework guides organizations through the improvement process (see Deming, 1993, p. 134; Lynch & Werner, 1992, p. 25).* It assumes that all three lead systems shown in Figure 8.1, particularly the performance measurement system, have been adequately established.

---

* Deming introduced plan-do-check-act (PDCA) in Japan in 1950 as the plan-do-study-act (PDSA) cycle. It later evolved to the more popular PDCA steps.

Plan (P)   PDCA   PDAI

In this phase the team must agree on an overall strategy to identify and implement improvements to its work system. The team gathers preliminary information on problems or opportunities in order to make two basic planning decisions.

- Who will be involved in the improvement process?
- What methodology will be used?

Both decisions are best made by answering a series of questions.

Who Will Be Involved?

1.   *Is the problem or opportunity a team issue?*

Not all problems or opportunities require a structured team attack. There are times when command decisions or consulting others for input only are appropriate. Making every problem a team problem could seriously hinder operations and damage performance. The decision on when to use a participative or team approach is very important. A team approach is warranted when the following conditions are present:

- The problem is particularly stubborn or long-standing, often with a string of failed improvement efforts.
- The identification of probable causes requires extensive data collection and broad, as well as in-depth, expertise.
- The solutions require substantial ownership by those involved to make them happen. In other words, you need to count on the principle that people don't resist their own ideas.

2.   *Who are the stakeholders and experts needed to be part of the improvement process?*

If each perpetual team in the organization is made up of interdependent members and, at least figuratively, can operate as an independent business, there should be little difficulty identifying who would be involved in the improvement process. In fact, the team's scorecard confirms its ownership of problems indicated by the performance measures. Sometimes, however, the improvement opportunities do not match up with the organization's natural teams. In these instances other forms of teams are warranted. Here are some of the generic types:

- Cross-functional teams including members of perpetual teams who have the necessary expertise to, on an ongoing basis, address problems and processes that cross natural team boundaries.
- Ad hoc teams or task forces that are formed to address a specific issue, often in an accelerated fashion, and then are disbanded.
- Subteams who address a part of a larger problem or process, then present their work to the whole team for decisions.

Once the team has decided if a particular improvement opportunity requires a team approach and exactly who will be members of that team, it must agree on a method to use to figure out a solution.

What Methodology Will Be Used?

1.   *What will work better—problem solving or process management?*

The vast array of available improvement tools and techniques can be conveniently classified into two basic methods or models: problem solving and process management. *Problem solving* is a method for systematically using facts and data to identify the root causes and match solutions to a problem. *Process management* is a method of defining the steps that transform specific inputs into outputs, the things that go wrong in that sequence, and the redesigned steps that eliminate these problems and streamline how the work is done. Both methods will be more fully described later in this chapter.

Although most teams are likely to use tools and techniques from both methods during the life of an improvement project, it is important to determine which model will direct the main improvement activities. The nature of the problem or opportunity will help decide.

These conditions point to problem solving as the driving method:

- There is a measurable gap between actual and expected performance on an accepted performance measure or other quantitative indicator.
- The problem is complex—the performance gap is intuitively due to multiple causes that seem likely to be difficult to prioritize and convert into workable solutions.

These conditions point to process management as the driving method:

- A gap on the team's key performance measure is suspected to be due to an inadequate or incorrect work process.
- There are several signs that one or a few vital processes are broken:

    Everyone seems to do the process, or their part of it, their own way.

    People "who know the system" have figured out ways to get things done by going around the process.

    There are no designated measures of how the process is working but generally people remark it is not effective or efficient.

    People are overwhelmed or burned out by the amount of effort and time required by the process.

    It's hard to say how long the process takes or how much it costs.

2. *Is a formal or informal improvement approach needed?*

Over the years, several variables that influence a team's level of success with performance improvement methods have emerged as common pitfalls. For instance, team members frequently are not sufficiently trained in the skills, steps, and tools that comprise the method. Teams also have difficulty conducting effective meetings—unproductive team behaviors and poor time management sidetrack use of the method. One often overlooked but prevalent barrier is the misapplication of the method in which teams attempt to force high-powered tools or techniques on a simple problem.

Team members can become frustrated when the solution or needed process change is evident but they sense they are obligated to follow several steps that they perceive are not necessary. They ask, for example, "Do we really have to list all causes and select those with a highest impact if we all agree on what we need to do?" The answer is often no. Likewise, teams may be confused about when to apply certain tools. For example, they might wonder if they should always use a Pareto diagram when prioritizing. Again, the answer is often no.

Just as not all problems require a team or participative approach, not all team problems require a highly structured, formal approach. A prudent team can employ a more informal improvement attack if certain conditions exist.

- The problem or process improvement opportunity is well defined and all team members describe the current situation rather consistently.
- The cost of the solution or process change is relatively low.
- The implications if the solution or process change fails are low risk—nothing very bad would happen.

To summarize thus far, the planning phase of the PDAI improvement cycle clarifies who will work on the problem and what method they will use to do it. Now for making performance improvement happen.

Do (D)   PDAI

In this phase the team implements three major interventions: goal setting, feedback, and problem solving or process management. Each intervention builds on the preceding one and requires a higher degree of effort. Each intervention can also produce its own breadth (number of performance measures improved) and depth (amount of change) of improvement. That is, goal setting alone could very well result in measurable improvements on some indicators simply by making expected performance standards clear. Feedback systems are even more likely to produce noticeable performance gains by letting people know how well they are performing against expectations. However, the outcome of problem solving or process management is what people typically think of as "success or failure" with respect to performance improvement. It's this third intervention that brings about the step-shift gains and breakthroughs that enable the team to contribute to the total organization's competitive position. This section will examine each of these three interventions in detail. But first, it's useful to look at a frequently misunderstood practice with application to two of these interventions as well as the development of measures—benchmarking.

Benchmarking—A Simple View. Volumes have been written about the concept of benchmarking. Granted, there is a technology to the practice of benchmarking that is beyond the scope of this book. Yet benchmarking has application to three major topics treated in this book.

First of all, in Chapter Three we described benchmarking as one method for identifying measures for hard-to-measure teams. It simply involves finding out who is the best at a "business" that is the same or comparable to that of your team—and then learning how they measure what they do. Benchmarking also has application to goal setting and problem solving or process management.

With respect to goal setting, benchmarking helps the team determine meaningful standards. It helps the team define what is possible. For example, a copy paper manufacturer collected data on the production rates of its competitors and was surprised to find its own productivity was significantly lagging on comparable products and machines. Various production targets were revised subsequently, changing maintenance tactics as well as capital spending.

Benchmarking can also reveal potential new ways of doing things in problem solving and process management interventions. This essentially involves comparing what you do to what the best do. In an interesting extension of this concept, a quality engineer at a producer of gas-fired barbecue grills examined the differences between two vendors who supplied fasteners, nuts, bolts, and so on. One supplier's parts bags consistently contained all the specified pieces while the other's frequently were missing parts. Knowing the company wanted to retain two vendors for various reasons and not having another local option, the engineer studied the suppliers' quality assurance methods. There were glaring differences between the high and low performers with regard to automation, packaging procedures, and inspection methods. With the knowledge and consent of the high performer, he helped the lower performer adapt and adopt some of the high performer's quality assurance practices—and the missing parts problem was nearly eliminated.

Whether used to identify measures, set goals, or assist in problem solving, the powerful simplicity of benchmarking is quite attractive. But there is a word of caution. Aspiring to the performance levels and practices of the best is not always recommended. Studies have shown that organizations that are novices to the improvement business may make things worse by trying to match the performance and practices of world-class performers (American Quality Foundation and Ernst & Young, 1992). It's not hard to see how setting overly ambitious targets can create a goal crisis.

Goal Setting. Many measurement systems include goals, often not distinguishing measures from targets set on those measures. These goals may be established by upper management and cascade down to the teams, much as the management perspective is used to help develop measures for some teams (see Chapter Three). Alternatively, in high-involvement systems, the measures and corresponding goals may be established at the team level, reviewed by management, and rolled up to create aggregate performance measures at higher organizational levels. In many cases, the goals are created by a blend of top-down and bottom-up approaches. Regardless of the direction of the flow, effective goal setting is governed by a special mind-set as well as several requirements and guidelines.

It turns out that a certain mind-set can promote successful goal setting—and understanding the elements of this mind-set is the starting point.

- *Team members must accept the principle of continuous improvement.* They cannot believe they will ever reach a satisfactory level of performance and be able to stop. They must embrace the notion that the team will never be good enough, that they must continue to get better and better.
- *The atmosphere must be high energy.* Goal setting should not be a casual affair. Expect to see some gnashing of teeth and questioning of suggested performance levels. You should also expect some excitement about achieving goals and helping advance the business. If there is no energy in the goal setting sessions, don't expect much commitment to the goals. In short, if there is no energy it would behoove the team leader or facilitator to positively charge the atmosphere by clarifying the link between team goal achievement and such benefits as improved competitive position and group or individual rewards.
- *Team members must agree to focus on goal achievement rather than goal failure.* Focusing on what will go wrong if they don't make their goal can negatively charge the atmosphere and

lead to setting low or easily achieved targets. The team must pledge, sometimes literally, to focus on what it will take to meet the performance levels needed to meet customer and business requirements.

After cultivating a positive and confident mind-set, the team is ready to review the requirements for good goals. Meaningful goals should meet the following criteria:

1. *Goals should be stated in specific, quantitative terms.* For example, a cost accounting team should aim to increase report accuracy to 99 percent rather than "do their best."

2. *Goals should be challenging.* A goal that represents a significant improvement over current levels will result in higher performance than an easy goal, provided the more difficult goal is considered attainable (Latham & Yukl, 1975).

3. *Goals should be set by team members, the performers responsible for achieving the goals.* Although research suggests that employee involvement in goal setting does not necessarily result in higher performance (Latham & Yukl, 1975), participation does increase ownership. Of course, the team will review many inputs (stakeholder expectations, historical data, and so on) when setting goals.

4. *Goals should be perceived as attainable.* Goals get their motivational value by association with positive consequences when they are achieved. Goals perceived as overly aggressive lose their power to mobilize team behavior. If this situation is widespread, organizations will experience a "goal crisis" in which employees ignore goals at best—and at worst take action to "counter control" the goal setters.

5. *Goals should be aligned with business strategy.* Team members will rise to the challenge when they see a direct relationship between a goal and a compelling business need. However, it is important to note that the general, albeit real, business

reason of "survival" is not very persuasive. It is simply too vague and often too remote to justify exceptional effort from team members.

Finally, with a positive mind-set established and the requirements of good goals understood, it's time for the team to formulate goals using five straightforward guidelines or steps.

Step 1: Agree on the language of goal setting. Far too often, organizations use a broad and imprecise vocabulary to communicate expectations. Goals, objectives, focus areas, priorities, key result areas, targets, and many other terms are liberally used throughout the goal-setting process. Although there is no one right way to define these terms, it is important for team-based organizations to specify the language they will use and stick to it. Figure 8.2 shows a model that has proven helpful. Naturally, terms can be mixed and matched to customize a language that fits the organization. It is important though, that all teams within an organization speak the same language.

Step 2: Review goal inputs for the most valuable improvement opportunities. Goals related to key result areas can come from many sources. For example, there are several vantage points from which to look for potential improvements in the key result area of quality. A team could aim to reduce returned goods, increase lot acceptance of incoming material, or decrease percent defective—the list of potential goals is virtually endless. Since a team seeks to energize its members around the most critical opportunities, it must sort out the common themes and arrive at a manageable set of goals. The following list presents the primary sources of improvement opportunities:

- Performance on current goals
  What goals has the team achieved that it wishes to take to the next level?

Figure 8.2   A Model of Goal-Setting Language

Key Result Areas	Goals	Measures	Targets
• The general performance area linked to business and customer requirements.	• Statements specifying improvement opportunities— usually start with verbs such as *increase* or *decrease*.	• Quantitative indicators that enable progress on a goal to be tracked.	• Specific numerical levels of performance we seek to achieve.

Example: Social Service Agency

Substance Abuse Prevention Services	→ Increase support for program funding	→ $ approved by legislature	→ $800,000 (20 percent increase over previous year)

What goals did the team miss and can't afford not to tackle again?

- Stakeholder expectations

What do external and internal customers need the team to improve?

What does management want the team to work on?

- Benchmark information

What levels of performance do the best achieve?

What processes or practices do the best use and how does the team compare?

- Team hunches and judgments

What does the team want to address?

What problems would the team like to fix?

- Historical data

What do the numbers say are the team's biggest opportunities?

What if the team could perform at its highest level ever achieved on a more consistent basis?

Step 3: Test selected goals. After a great deal of deliberation the team will select its main goals. Before proceeding to identify measures and corresponding targets, it is essential to make sure that the goals pass the test. An adaptation of the goal analysis method introduced over twenty years ago by Thomas Gilbert still serves well (Gilbert, 1978). It's called the ACORN test.

- A—*Accomplishment:* Does the goal represent a result, not a behavior or activity?
- C—*Controllable:* Does the team (the performers) have the majority of influence on the goal?
- O—*Overall Objective:* If the result were completely achieved, would anything else be expected with respect to the key result area? In other words, is this the "macro" goal or a subgoal?
- R—*Reconcilable:* If this goal were perfectly achieved, would it hinder or interfere with the accomplishment of other goals? That is, does it fit with other goals?
- N—*Numbers:* Can it be measured? Even if a measure doesn't currently exist, is there the capability to quantify the goal?

Step 4: Set measurable targets. Multiple targets should be set for each goal measure using the historical data referred to in Step 2. Both a short-term and long-term target are recommended. There are two basic reasons for multiple targets. For one, statistical laws maintain that performance on any given measure will vary from one reporting period to another due to random fluctuation. Although problem-solving and process management efforts described later in this chapter can reduce or shift this "normal variation," it will never be completely eliminated. The short-term target is used to account for the fact that there will be more such variation in the early stages of the improvement initiative than in the later stages. Second, experience reveals that management often sets or recommends rather ambitious levels of improvement. While these levels may be substantiated by careful competitive analysis, we have noted that setting world-class goals or targets can be harmful to many organizations (see discussion on benchmarking in this chapter). In addition, as noted earlier, goals perceived as unattainable lose their motivational value. Using management expectations or competitive requirements as the basis for long-term targets and allowing the team to participatively set more realistic short-term targets can do much to maintain the power of goals as well as to avoid a conflict that often seems to have no solution acceptable to all parties.

A reliable method to set targets in a consistent fashion across time and teams is presented in Figure 8.3 (Boyett & Conn, 1988b). Historical data is used to determine typical and best scores on a given measure. These scores are then used to extrapolate the short-term and long-term target.

Step 5: Adjust targets based on business and process knowledge. Historical data serves as a starting point for developing targets or goals. Sometimes, however, targets need to be adjusted based on knowledge of future conditions and events. The range of possible developments, of course, is quite wide—yet it is possible to list the most common ones:

- Planned modifications or upgrades to the technical system (equipment, materials, and so on) or social system (incentives, training, and so on)
- Forecast changes in product mix
- Anticipated improvements as the result of purposeful problem-solving or process management efforts

Once goals or targets are finalized the team is ready to keep score on how well it is meeting the expectations that it defined.

Providing Meaningful Feedback. All the effort spent on developing measures and setting goals would be wasted if performance information is not presented to team members in a timely and meaningful way. Performance feedback, the second intervention in the "Do" phase of the PDAI cycle, has a double function. First of

Figure 8.3 Target or Goal Setting Guide
(with production example)

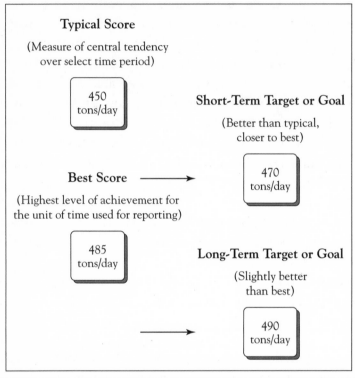

Typical Score

(Measure of central tendency
over select time period)

450
tons/day

Short-Term Target or Goal

(Better than typical,
closer to best)

470
tons/day

Best Score ⟶

(Highest level of achievement for
the unit of time used for reporting)

485
tons/day

Long-Term Target or Goal

(Slightly better
than best)

490
tons/day

Source: Joseph H. Boyett & Henry P. Conn, *Maximum Performance Management: How to Manage and Compensate People to Meet World Competition,* 1988, pp. 90–99. Copyright © 1995 by Glenbridge Publishing Ltd. Used by permission of the publisher.

all, numbers trending in the right direction or showing goal achievement reinforce the changes involved team members are making. The positive feedback confirms the behaviors team members believe are responsible for the noteworthy results. Second, scores not meeting expectations send the message that something must be done differently. Such feedback directs team members to identify and apply new behaviors—to solve problems or improve the process. Clearly, there is a potent influence on behavior when team members "know the score." In short, you cannot do well if you don't know how well you are doing. But how do you maximize the impact of this powerful intervention?

Create a Positive Climate for Feedback. Arguably the most important aspect of feedback concerns how it is perceived. The most common objection to a performance measurement and feedback system we encounter is that it will result in negative consequences. Team members envision being humiliated by comparisons to higher-performing teams, reprimanded for deteriorating performance, and frustrated by lack of progress. Although there is no better remedy for this thinking than to implement the system and not use it to punish, there are a few key norms based on W. E. Deming's fourteen points for management that can be established up front (Deming, 1982).

- *Feedback is desirable.* Remind the team that it has participated in identifying measures and setting goals to help maintain its own constancy of purpose—to achieve its overall mission and enhance the competitiveness of the organization. In that light, performance feedback is the next logical extension that supports the team's never-ending pursuit of purpose.

- *All information is useful.* Drive out fear and blame by demonstrating that performance below expectations is a signal for team problem solving and process improvement, not punishment. Also ensure that improvements and goal achievement are recognized. Positive and negative exceptions both receive energy; the former—the energy of celebration, the latter—the energy of figuring things out.

- *Disciplined learning will lead to improved results.* Help the team move quickly from disappointing results to the process that produced them. Looking for cause-effect relationships and process disconnects to see what's going on develops a learning orientation.

Allegiance to these norms or values will create an atmosphere in which feedback is a welcome addition to measures and goals.

Feedback Principles. A positive climate is a necessary but not sufficient condition for effective feedback. During the past three decades a feedback technology has emerged characterized by rather prescriptive principles.

1. *Review potential for detrimental side effects.*

Although a positive climate may be established, the possibility of negative side effects from competition within a team as well as between teams is very real. If group dynamics are such that a team is likely to unfairly make an individual a scapegoat for poor performance, you may wish to resolve this issue before initiating feedback. Similarly, if certain measures are perceived to foster an unhealthy rivalry between teams, minor changes in calculations or other aspects of the measures might help. For example, three separate shift-teams on the same machine complained that several measures on their scorecard not only created unproductive competition between the teams but also were susceptible to contamination by the preceding shift (that is, one shift could intentionally impede the performance of the next shift). Two changes were made: the housekeeping score was converted to a total machine score to which each shift contributed, and the production volume measure (influenced by product mix) was changed to an efficiency ratio that accounted for order difficulty. In summary, negative side effects should not prevent the use of feedback, these effects simply need to be surfaced and addressed. Ignoring them is not an option.

2. *Feedback should be precise and objective.*

Effective performance information is quantitative and specific to selected performance measures. Qualitative, editorial-style comments are typically not necessary. The numbers speak for themselves.

3. *Performance goals and other reference points should be employed.*

Current performance alone has little meaning. Showing current performance in relation to past performance (that is, baseline) as well as short-term and long-term goals puts the results in perspective and helps the team see what needs attention next.

4. *Provide feedback on a family of measures.*

Even though many teams search for the elusive single best indicator of team performance, we have never found it. If teams receive feedback on only one or two performance measures, team members may ignore other team business—or worse, sacrifice some areas of performance in favor of the few that are measured. Prior to the quality movement in the 1980s, many organizations almost exclusively measured internally driven production and cost. As a result, inferior products often reached the customer. The use of multiple measures or a balanced scorecard helps prevent this "tunnel vision" phenomenon (Kaplan & Norton, 1992).

5.   *Provide feedback to all levels of the organization.*

Participation of teams up and down the organization decreases the tendency to drift from objective performance information to subjective comments and increases the probability the feedback system will be maintained. More important, it establishes a mechanism of accountability for performance.

6.   *Use multiple feedback mechanisms.*

Studies of adult learning suggest that repetition and the use of different learning modalities (auditory, visual, and so on) greatly enhance people's ability to comprehend the messages delivered to them. Hence it is important to review performance information via team meetings, bulletin boards, electronic messages, signs, newsletters, and other information-sharing mechanisms. Any single mechanism has too many limitations.

7.   *The feedback format should be user-friendly.*

The limits of the human capability to process information are well documented. It's not arbitrary that the classic U.S. telephone number contained only seven digits. So more information is not better. In fact, less is often better. In addition, the data must be organized in such a way that the receivers can quickly attend to the information relevant to their team's performance. Generally speaking, use of tables should be minimized in favor of charts and graphs. Line graphs are particularly good because they reveal performance trends over time and easily depict baseline and goal levels. Several user-friendly formats were presented in earlier chapters.

8.   *Provide timely and frequent feedback.*

Feedback is most effective when it is provided immediately following a behavior. However, the results predominantly tracked in the measurement and feedback systems treated in this book are the product of multiple behaviors by teams of individuals. The performance scores for the most part are delayed. One rule of thumb is that there should be no more than a five-day delay between the end of the performance period and the publication of the data.

With respect to frequency, automation is making it much easier to provide both immediate and continuous feedback. More realistically, though, we prefer weekly but will settle for monthly feedback in the systems we design. Also keep in mind that the high variability (often called *noise*) present in daily or even weekly measures must sometimes be smoothed out with monthly computations.

9.   *Ensure the team fully understands the feedback data.*

The fact that the team has participated in both measurement development and goal setting helps—but it's no guarantee everyone will fully understand the feedback. Pilot test your scorecards, graphs, and so on before institutionalizing your feedback system. Make certain team members understand all aspects of the system well enough to both find mistakes in the data if errors are present and explain the feedback report or graph to someone outside the team. One feature we find in common among high-performing teams is they truly understand their performance measures, goals, and feedback materials.

10.   *Involve everyone in the feedback process.*

One of the best ways to get team members involved is to identify different "owners" for various measures in key result areas such as safety, quality, cost, and productivity. Prior to the team meeting, owners prepare the data for their specific graphs and distribute them to other team members. At the meeting the owners each encourage comments about the performance measures for which they are responsible.

11.   *Link performance feedback with the problem solving and reinforcement systems.*

As noted, positive performance exceptions should be recognized or otherwise rewarded. This topic will be discussed more fully in Chapter Nine. However, this is a good opportunity to point out that it would be difficult to review performance without recognizing those measures that are improving and meet or exceed target. Therefore, even though incentives and other reward systems may be formally connected to performance levels, don't forget to praise positive exceptions when reviewing the data.

However, negative performance exceptions must enter the problem solving and process management system. Performance feedback is the path to getting information needed to improve performance into the hands of those who do the work. But how do teams figure out how to change the way they work so as to get superior results?

Problem Solving and Process Management. Although some performance measures improve from either goal setting or feedback alone (or more likely from a combination of the two), generally most measures require more active intervention. The third and final intervention of the Do phase of the PDAI improvement cycle is the involvement of the team in problem solving or process management. In the Plan phase of the cycle, we pointed out that the many improvement tools and techniques could be classified into these two basic methods—which have more in common than one might think. They both consist of three important parts:

- *Skills:* Four basic skills apply equally to either model and form the foundation for both methods.

- *Steps:* A sequence of seven activities organize the team's thinking and behavior regarding improvement—the core of the methods.

- *Tools:* A set of techniques that support the use of facts and data throughout the seven-step process.

Figure 8.4 is an overview of the three parts, starting with the foundation skills displayed on the bottom.

A team should be able to make a seamless transition from feedback to one of these two improvement methods. The answers to the questions posed in the Plan phase determine which method to start with and drive the team's activities. The data from the measurement system merely feeds these methods. On the one hand, certainly a team can solve problems without a measurement system and, on the other hand, the system rarely contains enough data to solve a problem or improve a process—additional data collection is usually necessary. However, the measurement system, including measures, goals and feedback, provides greater discipline and focus in choosing worthy performance improvement projects.

An in-depth look at problem solving and process management is beyond the scope of this book. And you will probably deduce that there are a great number of bridges and similarities between the two models. For instance, in addition to the four shared skills, several tools are used in both methods. Flow diagrams and process mapping, for example, are very similar and are used in both methods. Tools are shown in Figure 8.4 under the method with which they are most often associated. Nonetheless, it's useful to get an overview of the two methods.

Four Common Skills. If someone were to ask, "What do high-performing teams do when they are solving problems or improving a process?" the answer lies with the four observable skills or behaviors that a team can engage in during a typical team meeting. These skills occur throughout the seven-step process. The tools simply complement the skills, particularly analysis. Therefore, if a team is not exhibiting any of those behaviors it is not using problem solving or applying process management.

• *Generating Ideas.* This is the production of ideas in quantity. It is typically used to list possible problems, probable causes, and potential solutions. Brainstorming is the most common form of the skill. There are, however, other techniques for generating ideas, including mind mapping, brain writing, and metaphor exercise.

• *Analyzing.* This is the use of a variety of tools to determine cause-effect relationships or how two or more variables might correlate. Problem solving and process management both require facts and data. Once the data is collected one must learn what the data

**Figure 8.4   Overview of the Three-Part Methods of Team
Problem Solving and Process Management**

P R O B L E M	PART 3: Tools (support)		P R O C E S S
	• Flow Diagrams ✗ • Process Map ✗ • Pareto Diagrams ✗ • Relationship Maps ✗ • Cause-and-Effect Diagrams ✗ • Variance Analysis ✗ • Scatter Diagrams ✗ • Cycle Time Evaluation ✗ • Check Sheets ✗ • Histograms ✗ • Charts and Graphs ✓		

	PART 2: Seven Steps (core)	

S O L V I N G	PRID²E² Model	Reengineering Model	M A N A G E M E N T
	1. Pinpoint the problem or opportunity	1. Select target process and define objectives	
	2. Review the situation	2. Map process "as is"	
	3. Identify major causes	3. Specify disconnects	
	4. D¹etermine best solutions	4. Reengineer process as it "should be"	
	5. D²rive implementation	5. Establish process measures	
	6. E¹valuate results	6. Evaluate process performance	
	7. E²stablish reliable methods	7. Standardize process	

PART 1: Four Common Skills (foundation)

Generating Ideas	Analyzing	Group Decision Making	Action Planning

⇧ START HERE ⇧

means, what patterns exist, and ultimately what causes lie at the root of the undesirable results.

- *Group Decision Making.* This is the behavior of choosing among several alternatives. Often considered a difficult skill by team members, in its simplest form it is typically a structured voting and ranking procedure. For example, one method for prioritizing or pruning a list of ideas when there are five to fifteen team members is to give each person a specified number of votes calculated by dividing the total number of ideas by five and adding one. Team members can each place all their votes on one idea or distribute them any way they wish. More complex decision-making procedures include use of decision matrices and the Nominal Group Technique. Consensus decisions are the most challenging to reach, as they require all team members to agree or at least buy in to a particular alternative. Reducing the alternatives with voting and ranking helps set the stage for the in-depth discussion involved in reaching consensus. Decision criteria, like those in decision matrices, are almost always needed to arrive at consensus.

• *Action Planning.* This is the class of behaviors that convert chosen ideas into specific assignments (that is, who does what by when). Action plans can range from a simple list of action items to more complex timelines or project plans using Gantt and PERT charts.

Of course, numerous interpersonal skills are required for team effectiveness as well. Active listening, assertiveness, and conflict resolution are the primary ones needed by all team members in addition to the four basic skills.

Seven Steps. The seven steps of each method are the core of the improvement effort. The structure ensures the team gets to the root of the problem or process variance in order to fix it permanently. Many companies have standard problem-solving processes for their teams to follow. The Xerox six-step process was described in Chapter Five. We will first describe the seven-step problem-solving method we refer to by the acronym P-R-I-D^2-E^2, which has been successfully used by a wide variety of teams in many organizations, then do the same with the reengineering model used in process management. Both sets of steps are shown in Figure 8.4.

The PRID^{2}E^2 Model.
Step 1: *Pinpoint a problem or improvement opportunity.*

The team begins by brainstorming problem areas or opportunities to improve. These problems should be within the team's own scope of responsibility. As the team members list these problems or opportunities, they should provide supporting data, where available, to highlight the needed improvement. The performance measurement system meets this need quite well. There are several approaches to choosing the problem or opportunity to address. One approach is to consider three sources of direction in selecting worthy improvement targets (see Figure 8.5). In this approach, management priorities are clarified by asking senior managers what improvement opportunities come to mind when they think of a particular team. These priorities are not shared with the team members until after they brainstorm their own concerns. Teams are also asked to review their performance measures to find the biggest gaps between current performance and their goals or targets. Figuratively speaking, the most worthy problems or opportunities should be those common to all three views (that is, the intersection of the circles).

A second approach prescribes that the team choose any problem its members wish, preferably the easiest. The assumption is the

Figure 8.5   Three Sources of Direction in Selecting Improvement Targets

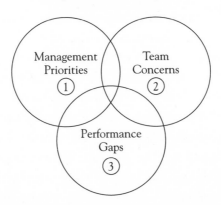

Source: Don Schilling, "Building a Team Measurement and Feedback System to Drive Performance." In *Action Developing High-Performance Work Teams,* Volume 1, Jack J. Phillips, series editor. Copyright 1998 by the American Society for Training & Development, Alexandria, VA. Reprinted with permission. All rights reserved.

team will succeed, gain confidence, and tackle increasingly more difficult and valuable improvements.

A third approach is based on the Theory of Constraints as popularized by E. M. Goldratt (see Goldratt & Cox, 1986). According to the theory, constraints occur when variability becomes linked to interdependence. Constraints are often identified by excessive wasted time stemming from unfinished product or service piling up at particular points in the process—and from repeated efforts to compensate for the problem. Most constraints are the result of outmoded policies and procedures.

Regardless of the approach, the outcome of Step 1 is a clear statement of the problem or opportunity agreed on by the team.

Case Study: University Graduate Program Revisited

The university graduate program case from Chapter Three presents a good example of the application of the Theory of Constraints. Recall that this team was using a thirty-year-old admissions policy that brought in large numbers of students via low standards. Consequently, there was a great deal of variability among the students in terms of motivation and ability. The constraint was a function of this variability and the fact that a student's progress depended on clearing a series of hurdles such as core courses, comprehensive exams, and a thesis. One symptom of the constraint was the wasted time in team meetings discussing students who were performing poorly. These meetings would often last two to three hours—and yet the team did not get around to discussing how to improve opportunities for the high-performing students. The other symptom was that many students did not graduate on schedule. The problem was correctly identified as excessive variability. The solution was to raise admission standards, which reduced the variability of incoming students. As a result, both symptoms disappeared, and the team experienced a major success. The benefits of that success have lasted for several years.

Step 2: Review the situation.

The team studies the current conditions or state associated with the problem from several perspectives. Members are likely to flow chart the process as well as answer key questions such as these:

- What exactly is happening or not happening, stated in quantitative terms?
- Where and when does it happen?
- Are there any patterns to its occurrence or nonoccurrence?

The outcome of this step is a goal statement accompanied by measures and corresponding targets. For example, the goal may be to reduce machine downtime, measured as number of minutes per day. The target, based on a hypothetical baseline of 110 minutes per day, could be 60 minutes per day depending on other facts and data collected about the situation.

Step 3: Identify major causes.

The next step takes the team into a search for the root causes of the problem. This step, like Step 1, begins by brainstorming or otherwise generating all the possible causes of the problem. Cause-and-effect and affinity diagrams are useful here. Next the team uses group decision-making skills to reduce the list to the most likely causes.

Some teams use the technique of the "five whys" to determine the root causes. Simply put, the team asks why the problem happens. The answer gives the first-order cause and the team in turn asks why it occurs. The team continues to ask why until it has followed the whole chain of causation back to the most basic factor.

Check sheets are then often used to collect data that validate the root causes. In addition, the team may need to employ outside experts to help identify probable causes when the problem is highly technical. Combining the team's expertise with that of an expert may quickly lead to the root causes of the problem.

Step 4: Determine the best solutions.

A member of a highly successful team once said, "If you truly identify the root causes of a problem, the solutions jump out and hit you right in the face." There's no question that there should be a line of sight between causes and chosen solutions. But there is more than one way to skin a cat. Teams, therefore, typically also brainstorm solutions and then select those that best address the causes.

Step 5: Drive implementation of the solutions.

Teams often present their recommended solutions only to watch them wither away and die. It's almost as if presenting the team's solution is the end of the process. But it is far from the end. In this step the team mobilizes for action. Using their action planning skills, the members clearly specify an implementation strategy and timeline in the format of who will do what, when. The team then implements the plan, regularly following up on progress—or lack thereof. At this point, persistence is crucial.

Step 6: Evaluate the results.

Here team members ask: "Did we achieve our goal?" This question is answered by comparing new data to the targets established in Step 2. Perhaps the targets have not yet been achieved but measurable improvement is evident. The data leads the team to debug certain aspects of the solutions, make midstream adjustments, and drive implementation of the modified solutions.

Step 7: Establish reliable methods.

Once the results are satisfactory and all major corrections to the solutions have been completed, the team must standardize and institutionalize the new ways of doing things. This starts with documenting new practices and procedures for future use in training new team members.

Case Study of a Duracell Chemical Processing Team

This team at a Duracell plant mixes and blends the powder that goes into alkaline batteries, so it is known as the powder system team. When the team began using its new measurement system, it decided to go for an early success. The team members focused on the performance measure where they thought they could have the most impact. As described in Chapter One, they chose "press utilization"—the machine speed of their internal customer, the press room, the next group downstream in the manufacturing process. The press room presses the powder into rings that constitute the outer core of the battery. Press utilization is a function of the consistency of the material produced by the powder system. The more consistent the powder, the faster the presses can run (up to their maximum speed or 100 percent utilization). The problem was that the powder mixture was somewhat inconsistent, therefore the press room team had to keep adjusting its machines to accommodate the variability in the material, thus reducing the machine speeds.

After identifying this problem, the powder system team collected historical data on press utilization, finding that the figure averaged 74 percent. With the help of a chemical engineer, the team determined that the formulation of the powder created clumps in the powder. The engineer developed and installed a new formulation that produced powder of equal quality without the clumps. This produced a sudden improvement, up to an average of 80 percent. Subsequently, the team brainstormed ideas to further improve the consistency of the powder. For example, one employee suggested that he could manually shake the grates that sift the powder every hour. This resulted in fewer clumps in the powder. Through the brainstorming process, the team suggested hundreds of possible improvements over the course of the next eight months. It developed action plans, complete with who was responsible to implement those suggestions that were approved by management. Those ideas produced a steady improvement, until press utilization eventually reached 92 percent (see Figure 8.6). The team members called this a "home run," and it increased their confidence level for tackling harder problems in the future.

The Reengineering Model. Michael Hammer and James Champy first introduced reengineering in the early 1990s largely because traditional improvement tools, including the PRID^{2}E^2 problem-solving model described in this book, were not resulting in the ten-fold gains many organizations needed to be competitive (see Hammer & Champy, 1993). The TQM movement had apparently played out and its slower, evolutionary mode seemed poorly matched to the quickening pace of the global economy. In addition, statistical quality tools, as well as the techniques employed by other schools of thought (such as synchronous management or sociotech redesign), worked well in manufacturing but not so well in gray- and white-collar improvement initiatives. Since then, reengineering practices have made major contributions to the competitive position of many organizations. The following steps are a hybrid of the best practices in process improvement and management.

Step 1: Select target process and define objectives.

Identifying the right processes to reengineer can be a difficult task for an organization. Typically a team may own or play a significant role in tens of processes. Since most process work is performed

Figure 8.6   Performance Data for Powder System Team Efforts

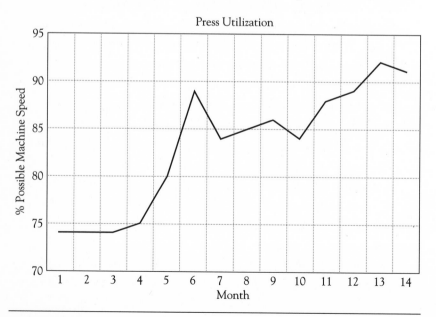

horizontally across the organization, the Plan phase of the PDAI cycle will most likely identify the need for a cross-functional team to redesign a process. In fact, most reengineering teams are selected based on their match to processes targeted for a fix. Typically the most strategically important processes are those that come into contact with customers—you know, the people who pay the bills. The order fulfillment and product development processes are examples of processes with major impact on customers. Processes that significantly affect everyday performance of internal operations come next on the importance scale. Various production or maintenance processes (for example, work order scheduling) are examples of these.

Earlier in this chapter we covered some of the signs that a process is broken. Essentially the signs fall into three categories of observations.

- No one can quantify the performance of the process.
- People are circumventing the process.
- Although there may be no specific information, the process clearly takes too much time, effort, and money to perform.

Once a process has been selected for improvement and a team formed to drive the effort, the process objectives must be defined. This is usually a statement specifying the outputs and their quantity, quality, cost, and timeliness requirements. For example, the objective of a maintenance work order system might be defined as equipment repairs and modifications identified, planned, scheduled, and completed to maximize uptime.

Step 2: Map the process "as is."

Starting with a macro-block diagram, the team charts the major process steps as currently designed. This may not be the way they are currently performed, but problems of omission or commission are identified in Step 3. The team maps the process to the level of specificity required to clearly understand what is done by whom, and in what order. Relationship maps are sometimes required.

Step 3: Specify disconnects.

Here the team identifies what goes wrong in the process. There could be a host of problems or variances:

- Duplicate steps or work
- Unnecessary, non-value-adding steps
- Excessively time-consuming activities
- Manual work that might be easily automated
- Overly complex steps
- Steps that could be combined
- Steps or activities in the wrong order
- Lack of compliance with certain steps
- Steps frequently resulting in waste or rework
- Steps that result in user or customer complaints
- Missing steps that are typically added by performers

A structured variance analysis is often used to identify where high-frequency, high-impact problems are likely to occur.

Step 4: Reengineer the process as it "should be."

This step may be a bit misleading. The variance or disconnect analysis may reveal that the process does not need to be redesigned. "Not all processes need to be reengineered," say Geary Rummler and Alan Brache (1995, p. 124). Some processes need only minor adjustments. Still others require only clarification—performers simply have not been informed about how the process works or they have not fully understood communications and training regarding the process.

Regardless of the magnitude of the redesign, the new state or "should be" process must be mapped to the same level of specificity as the team used for the "as is" process.

Step 5: Establish process measures.

Insofar as the first few steps focused on analyzing and improving the process, Step 5 is the first step in organizing a process management system. The aim of process management, in this context, is to ensure that variances and disconnects do not creep back into the process. To this end, process measures must be developed to reflect either the extent to which the process produces the desired outputs, the degree to which certain steps have been performed, or both.

Step 6: Evaluate process performance.

The team must make certain that the process is monitored and continually improved. The first part is to arrange regular reviews of the process measures to determine if the process is meeting customer and business requirements. More specifically, "Is the process meeting its objectives?" as defined in Step 1. The second part is to establish a corrective action process that converts the team's data review into improvement actions.

Step 7: Standardize the process.

At this point the process has been redesigned, documented, deployed, and debugged. It is important to once again document the process following minor adjustments and disseminate the information to the performers involved. This debug-document-deploy cycle never ends.

Case Study of a Member Enrollment Process

The vice president of operations at a locally owned chain of fitness centers in a Southeastern metropolitan area contracted with the second author to conduct management training for the twenty-seven members of the top management team. The four-day class consisted of training in communication, problem solving, and performance management. But a funny thing happened in the class.

On the first day, class discussions kept coming back to the hunch that new membership revenues were being lost because of a cumbersome enrollment process. So a ninety-minute period was set aside in each of the last three class sessions to follow the process improvement and management steps explained in this chapter. The "as is" process map and analysis of disconnects revealed the follow-ing points:

- The enrollment process typically took nearly three hours.
- No less than four employees interacted with the prospective member.
- Over half a dozen forms had to be completed by staff or the potential new member.
- In general, the process was more like an orientation than an enrollment.
- Prospective customers often remarked about the length of the process, often saying they had other appointments and would return another day.

The process was redesigned in a little more than an hour. Here are some of the changes in the "should be" process:

- After being greeted by the front desk personnel, the prospective customer was escorted to the Health Coordinator with whom they would remain.
- The facility tour was reduced from approximately an hour to twenty minutes, unless there were special interests.
- With the exception of credit applications, only one form was used.

Quantitative results of the before and after type were not reli-ably collected. However, process cycle time was cut in half, to between an hour and an hour and a half. In addition, staff reported that few, if any, prospects left before enrollment was completed due to time conflicts. Simplify, simplify, simplify!

Brief descriptions of the tools and techniques of problem solv-ing and process management are shown in Table 8.1 and Table 8.2 respectively. A full treatment of these tools cannot be presented

Table 8.1   Overview of Basic Problem Solving Tools

Tool	Usage
Flow Diagram	Organizes information about a process in a sequential and graphical manner. Primarily shows inputs, steps, decision points, and outputs.
Check Sheet	A format for recording and organizing information, usually numerical data. Often used to collect data verifying likely causes. Can also be used to present itemized text information such as procedures.
Pareto Diagram	A means for prioritizing problems or causes. It rank orders variables to show the relative contribution of each.
Cause-and-Effect Diagram	A tool for identifying, organizing, and displaying causes that might lead to a specified effect or problem. Causes are typically organized in the categories of people, equipment, materials, methods, and information.
Histogram	A bar-type chart for displaying the distribution of a characteristic or variable measured many times, typically thirty to fifty.
Scatter Diagram	A graph that displays how one variable changes when another changes, that is, it shows how one variable is related to another.
Graphs and Charts	Many types are available—bar chart, pie chart, waterfall chart, and so on—used for a variety of purposes. The *run chart* is a common graph that displays performance over time. Its more sophisticated cousin, the *control chart*, shows performance over time as well as the state of control of a process.

Table 8.2 Overview of Basic Reengineering Tools

Tool	Description
Process Map 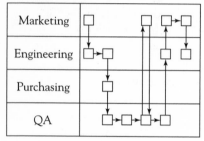	Similar to flow chart. Usually starts at "macro" level and proceeds to increasingly more detailed levels. Used to study the process, particularly opportunities to streamline by reducing or combining steps.
Relationship Map — Marketing, Engineering, Purchasing, QA	Basically a stratified flow chart that shows when a process crosses department or team boundaries. Each step appears in the row of the department or team that performs it. It is used primarily to detect complex processes with many hand-offs.
Variance Analysis — Variance / Major Causes / Where Detected / Who Fixes; 1, 2, 3, 4	Variances are things that go wrong in the process, such as failures to meet customer-driven quality requirements or deviations from normal operating performance. They are usually identified by mapping the process first and then answering questions about who detects and controls them.
Cycle Time Evaluation — Step / Activity Type / Time Spent; 1 O, 2 D, 3 O, 4 T	A method for assessing how long a total process takes from input to output, as well as the time consumed by steps within the process. The activity type of each step can be specified to better understand the process (for example, O—operations, D—delay).

here and the reader is reminded that more complete information can be found in many works. *Team Management* and *The Advanced Team Guide* from the Miller/Howard Consulting Group are particularly helpful.*

Assess (A) –

The long journey through the PDAI improvement cycle is nearing an end. The third phase, Assess, is often mistaken as a duplication of the evaluate step (Step 6) in the problem solving and reengineering methods. But this phase involves assessing much more than the success or failure of a particular improvement project. Here, the organization assesses the collective results of all the teams. It's a time to evaluate the progress toward the vision of measurement-driven, high-involvement teams.

There are certainly a great many qualitative judgments to be made based on some key questions, a self-assessment if you will.

1. Are most people involved in team meetings that review performance and actively pursue improvement opportunities?
❑ Yes   ❑ No

2. Do the teams have sufficient performance information to select and resolve improvement opportunities that are truly tied to the organization's strategy to advance the business?
❑ Yes   ❑ No

3. Do the teams employ standardized improvement methods such as the PRID^{2}E^2 problem solving model or reengineering model?
❑ Yes   ❑ No

4. Do team meetings occur regularly as scheduled?
❑ Yes   ❑ No

---

*These guides are available from the Miller/Howard Consulting Group, Inc., 750 Hammond Drive, Building 12, Suite 200, Atlanta, GA 30328.

5. Do improvement activities actually result in documented changes to the work system?

❑ Yes   ❑ No

6. Have team improvement efforts collectively led to measurable gains in key result areas at the organizational level?

❑ Yes   ❑ No

True to the values and principles of team performance measurement, there are also a number of indicators that shed light on the key questions as well as offer their own insights about the organization.

- Percent of employees on one or more teams
- Percent of teams with an active improvement project
- Percent of improvement projects at various steps in the problem solving or reengineering methods
- Percent of team meetings held as scheduled
- Percent of improvement projects showing improvement over baseline
- Percent of improvement projects achieving or exceeding short-term goal or target
- Percent of improvement projects achieving or exceeding long-term goal or target

Once qualitative and quantitative information is collected on the state of the high-involvement team system, the organization is poised to improve.

Improve (I)

The final phase of the improvement cycle is firmly rooted in the principle of continuous improvement, an aspect of the mind-set discussed in relationship to goal setting. But a few more comments are in order concerning this most important principle.

Continuous improvement requires continuous learning. An organization must learn from what went right and what went wrong to enhance its capability. In this phase, people renew their commitment to performance-driven involvement, ensure gains are maintained, develop plans to overcome weaknesses in the team measurement and improvement systems, and recognize their successes.

Summary

Measurement provides a starting point for the performance improvements that advance an organization's competitive position. Performance measurement, together with leadership and training, are the lead systems that enable team improvement activities. Reinforcement, the trailer system, provides motivation to pursue valuable improvements. The improvement methodology used by the team is the core system—the means by which team members figure out how to do things differently.

The PDAI improvement cycle guides teams through the improvement process. In the Plan phase (P), the team determines who will be involved and what specific method will drive its improvement activities, problem solving or process management. The Do phase (D) is the heart of the cycle and includes three interventions: setting goals, establishing feedback, and implementing changes identified through team problem solving or process management. There are mind-sets, principles, and other guidelines that govern the effective application of each intervention, and each can produce its own results. But it's the third intervention that typically yields the most significant improvements in performance.

The team problem-solving and process management methods consist of three parts: skills, steps, and tools. The team skills (such as generating ideas, group decision making, and so on) are common to the improvement process and many of the tools and techniques (such as flow diagrams, process maps, and so on) are used with both methods. The seven steps of problem solving are outlined by the PRID²E² model and focus the team on identifying root causes and the corresponding solutions to well-defined problems. The seven steps of process management are enumerated in the reengineering model, which directs the team to map a process it perceives to be broken, specify the things that go wrong, and redesign the process to eliminate those problems and streamline the work. Case studies are presented to illustrate both models.

The third phase, Assess (A), requires the organization to evaluate the activities and results of all teams. Qualitative judgments as well as quantitative indicators are examined to determine the extent to which teams are measuring and improving performance. The final phase, Improve (I), uses the assessment findings to formulate a plan to continually enhance the organization's capability through measurement-driven high-involvement teams.

Assessing Your Team

1. Using the goal-setting guidelines presented in this chapter, select a measure from your team's measurement system that needs improvement. Set a short-term and long-term target for this measure.

2. Using this same measure, determine the performance improvement method—problem solving or process management—the team should use to reduce the gap between current performance and target performance. Develop a timeline that your team might use to complete the seven steps for the method you choose.

3. Evaluate your team's feedback system. How does it measure up against the eleven principles outlined in this chapter? More important, what is the typical response to positive and negative exceptions highlighted by the feedback?

4. Identify a broken process that involves your team and one or two other teams. Form a cross-functional team to reengineer the process. Discuss the team's reactions as it proceeds

through the prescribed steps. To what extent do those involved understand how the "as is" process is designed to work? How did the major disconnects or problems evolve? Does the team need to completely redesign the process or simply make a few minor adjustments? What is the team's level of confidence that the "should be" process will be properly implemented and maintained?

5. Assess your team's general climate for performance improvement. Are team members motivated to engage in problem solving or are they afraid and defensive when problems are identified? How disciplined are the team's problem-solving and process-management efforts? Is the team empowered, within the appropriate boundaries, to make decisions that drive solutions? Based on your answers to these questions, formulate a development plan for your team so that performance measurement will lead to improvements that contribute to the organization's success.

Chapter Nine

Fueling Performance

Performance-Based Team Incentives

A manager is talking with her team leader:

Diane: We started teams, we reorganized, empowered people to make decisions, we have a steering committee, team training, team charters, and structured team meetings—yet the team members still don't seem to want to take ownership for their part of the business. They still act like employees.

Sam: That's the way it is in my team. If we don't make our productivity goals, it is still viewed as management's problem. I guess if we want the team members to act like business partners, we have to treat them like business partners.

Once an organization has established solid measurement systems for its teams, and the teams use those measures to solve business problems, what is needed to keep these systems working? Research indicates that the combination of team measurement, feedback, and problem solving can have a 10 percent to 50 percent impact on a team's performance in a few months. (See, for example, Jones, Buerkle, Hall, Rupp, & Matt, 1993; Jones, Powell, & Roberts, 1990; and Pritchard, Jones, Roth, Stuebing, & Ekeberg, 1988.) Therefore, it is worthwhile to consider what is necessary to keep these systems operating successfully in the long run. Incentives can successfully fuel the measurement system for the long haul. There are several different types of incentive systems, but— in keeping with the focus of this book—this chapter will only address performance-based team incentives.

Experience has shown that the keys to a successful incentive program are alignment and buy-in. Consider shooting a gun at a target. The target represents the business strategy, the front sight of the gun is the team strategy and the rear sight is the team's performance measures, as in Figure 9.1. To take the analogy further, the bullet is the team's performance and the gunpowder is the incentive. If the sights and the target are not aligned, the performance will miss the mark. Spending more money on powder won't solve the problem. If there is no buy-in, they won't take the shot. Therefore, you need to do the work up front to ensure both alignment and buy-in.

Ongoing Incentives

In spite of their best efforts to promote teams, many organizations use an individually based pay system. Unfortunately, this sends a strong message that the company is less than serious about teams. Think of it as "rewarding A while hoping for B." In fact, a survey by the American Compensation Association (Gross, 1997b) found that between 20 percent and 30 percent of team failures were due

Figure 9.1   Lining Up the Sights

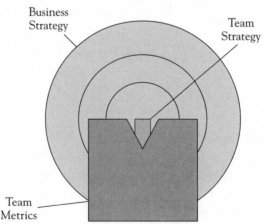

Business Strategy

Team Strategy

Team Metrics

to lack of team-based incentives. Realizing this, some companies have installed team-based incentive systems as part of their team-implementation effort. A recent survey by the Hay Company found that 12 percent of companies used team compensation and 39 percent were considering implementing team-based pay. A widely respected researcher and consultant, Edward Lawler, presents a good overview of team-based incentives in which he states, "The most powerful way to motivate team performance is to establish objectives and metrics for successful team performance then link rewards to team success" (Lawler, 1999).

Most consultants advise that incentives should be the last component of the team intervention. This is sound advice. Incentives should be implemented conservatively for several reasons:

- Incentives have the greatest variability of any intervention (Guzzo, Jette, & Katzell, 1985). Sometimes incentives improve performance, sometimes they fail, but they often create unintended consequences.

- It is much easier to add incentives then it is to take them away. This is an understatement. It is extremely upsetting to people when a company takes away financial and other tangible incentives. The negative impact lasts for years, and it has the strongest effect on high performers.

- An organization needs to know ahead of time how much money will be required for the incentive system as well as how it will be funded.

- Teams need time to establish their measurement system and problem-solving processes before they are ready for incentives. If they don't have well-established problem-solving processes, under the pressure of incentives they often degenerate into blaming each other instead of looking for ways to improve.

In spite of these cautions, incentives are necessary in the long run. For teams to function like business partners, they need to be treated like business partners. To paraphrase the movie *Jerry McGuire*, "Show them the money." It is logical that if teams are helping solve business problems, they should share in the rewards.

The Process

The process for developing incentives simply extends the measurement system development process with two more steps, to determine the funding mechanisms and the payment scheme. Therefore, the incentive design would follow this sequence:

1. Understand business strategy
2. Determine customer needs
3. Identify team strategy
4. Determine areas in which to measure performance
5. Brainstorm measures and examine available measures
6. Select best measures of team performance
7. Review by management
8. Test measures with real data
9. Make modifications
10. Develop feedback reports
11. Set up regular feedback and problem solving sessions (for example, monthly)
12. Determine funding mechanisms
13. Attach incentives to the measurement system

Funding Mechanisms

Something needs to fund the incentive system so that an incentive will be available when the team earns it. This funding mechanism should be designed so that it is affordable to the organization.

Nonfinancial Incentives

Since the first eleven steps of the process have already been covered, we will begin with determining how to provide the incentives. Most incentives will be financial, but a few situations may require nonfinancial incentives. The best nonfinancial incentive seems to be time off (with pay). This incentive works well in nonprofit organizations and the amount of time off can be calculated much like financial incentives. One difference is that financial incentives are calculated to the dollar, while time off is usually calculated in half-day blocks. Additionally, with time off, team members have to take their earned time off as the work allows, rather than everyone taking it at once. Clearly, if a team consistently earns time off, it should get its time off and not have its manpower reduced.

Financial Incentives

Most team incentive programs are fueled by money. The beauty of these systems is that teams are rewarded for treating their work like it is their own business. Many team incentive programs are also self-funding in that they pay for themselves. The money may come from five sources: productivity, cost-of-quality, budget management, profit, and cost-of-living raises. Many companies establish a productivity goal of a certain dollar value per labor hour. Exceeding this goal can fund the incentive system. Not all of the excess should go into the incentive system, however, since there are other improvement efforts beyond the scope of teams that contribute to the productivity improvement. Typically, 25 percent to 50 percent of the productivity improvement over and above the company goal may be put into the incentive system.

Cost-of-quality presents another funding opportunity. Premium freight costs and shipping costs for customer returns can fund an incentive program, because these are expenses paid to keep customers happy when something goes wrong with an order. As teams solve quality problems and problems with the order process, these costs will drop. Accounts receivable provides a similar funding mechanism, because unhappy customers tend to delay paying their bills. When this happens, a company may have to borrow money against its accounts receivable to maintain its cash flow. The fees and interest charges on these loans can fund the incentive program. This funding mechanism has the added advantage of aligning the team with customer needs. As customer service improves, the team's potential earnings grow. Additional means of funding from cost-of-quality include scrap, rework, and seconds.

Some teams manage a budget, such as that for parts and materials. The Xerox service team discussed in Chapter One and Chapter Five uses money saved from the parts budget to fund its incentive program. To save money on parts, it can return unused parts for credit, use only the parts truly needed for repairs, and keep up with inventory to avoid rush orders and premium freight costs. This is the team's budget, and it gets managed like a business.

Some organizations will take a category of profit, such as operating profit, to fund the incentive program. In these programs, the company makes a logical link between team performance and profitability. Provided that the team measurement systems are aligned with the business strategy, greater team performance should result in greater operating profit. It should be understood that this link is less direct than the link to cost-of-quality, since external factors can also affect profitability.

In some organizations cost-of-living increases fund (or partially fund) the incentive program. Many consider this a poor funding mechanism since there is no "win" in it for team members. They are only earning back what they would have gotten anyway. Such a program may backfire and only increase the sense of entitlement with regard to the incentive program. This can be seen when teams set low goals or choose measures on which they know they can achieve high scores.

It is possible to partially fund a successful incentive program with part of the cost-of-living raise, provided additional funding comes from other sources such as productivity, cost-of-quality, or budget management. As long as the team members can make more money than they would have with just the cost-of-living increase, the program may be considered fair. With each of these funding mechanisms, both the team members and the company must win if the program is to succeed.

Attaching Incentives

The two questions teams will probably ask regarding incentives are "how much" and "how soon." Incentive programs average 5 percent to 10 percent of base pay. However, in the early stages, a company might begin conservatively, say at 4 percent, then add to that as the plan succeeds. There are many successful cases with a potential incentive of $1000 per team member per year. This is on the low side, and the company should plan to add to this amount in the second and third years of the program. If teams are earning the maximum, the company will probably want to raise the teams' goals. This is a good time to "sweeten the pot." If the company wants teams to become business partners, the incentive pool should increase as the company succeeds.

The second question, "how soon," involves both the frequency of the incentive payouts and when the payouts should begin following the development of the measurement system. Quarterly payouts seem feasible for many companies. This balances the need of the teams to get paid frequently with the accounting department's need to calculate the funding amounts. Team members report that getting the incentive payment once a year or every six months is not frequent enough to motivate them. Doubtless there are exceptions, especially if the teams know the incentive they earn will really be paid, but it's easy for the "what have you done for me lately?" syndrome to start eating into team performance if the payments are too far apart.

Regarding the length of time after the measurement system is established, six months seems ideal. It gives the teams a chance to develop their problem-solving skills and gives the company enough data to forecast the cost of the incentive system. Obviously, if the company promised an incentive system within a year, and it is already the third quarter, the incentive system will have to begin as soon as the measures are developed. The timing in this case leads to teams' wanting to choose measures on which they will do well. It also leads teams to set goals they know they can meet. Neither of these approaches helps to develop a sound measurement system, since the objective is to set challenging goals on measures that capture the business strategy and the customer needs.

Spot Rewards

Many team successes can be amply rewarded without creating a new pay structure. Spot rewards are very useful in the following situations:

- Rewarding an outstanding one-time achievement, such as solving a long-standing problem or providing truly remarkable customer service.
- Rewarding a non–team member's contribution to the team's success.
- Recognizing the successful completion of an effort by a project team.
- Acknowledging that an individual or a team has gone above and beyond the performance norm.
- Reaching a milestone in the company's success.

Both noncash and cash rewards can work. Noncash rewards, when done correctly, enhance the sense of pride that team members already feel as partners in the business. Spot cash rewards should not be overlooked, because they send a strong message of appreciation. A good situation for using them is when someone from outside the team helps the team meet its goal. If the team will subsequently receive a financial bonus, a cash spot reward for a support person might be appropriate.

Generally, the most effective noncash rewards engage the employees socially. Lunches, dinners, and sporting events have all been used successfully. One of the most effective noncash rewards is "Family Day" where employees' families come to the workplace for lunch and entertainment. During this time, team members show their families around the workplace and point out the work processes for which they are responsible. Team members take extra pride in showing their families that what they do is important to the success of the business.

Pride and recognition are very powerful—but eventually most teams are going to want tangible rewards, such as money or time off with pay. Awards of appreciation become increasingly difficult to administer in the long run. It is also difficult for nonfinancial rewards to remain rewarding over time. After all, how many pens and caps does a person really need?

Even when using an ongoing system of tangible rewards, recognition plays an important role. One military team had been earning a half-day to a full day per month off with pay for six months. The team's performance consistently exceeded the challenging goals it had set. During one of their meetings, team members seemed dissatisfied with their incentive. They were pleased with time off but they were bothered by the fact that "the old man hasn't been back here for months." The "old man" they referred to was the colonel in charge of their area of the base. Since this team was doing so well, the colonel was focusing his attention on other units. An arrangement was made for the colonel to stop by and review the team's performance, which was posted on graphs around the work area. He came to the next meeting, explained why he hadn't been in their shop, looked over their performance graphs, and gave them recognition (an "attaboy," in military terms). It was very powerful. Believe it or not, it seemed to be more reinforcing than the time off with pay. A valuable lesson was learned that day: never underestimate the importance of personal recognition.

Special Considerations

Financial rewards or time off with pay can be easily connected to a team's performance measurement system via the composite score. However, as stated earlier, incentives can be tricky. Several issues require resolution to ensure success.

- *Teams have a natural tendency to focus on their own work to the exclusion of other teams.* Incentives can aggravate this problem. If teams need to cooperate, it is imperative that they share at least one measure with each other. Otherwise the incentive encourages them to compete. In the example of the assembly team shown in Table 9.1, the productivity measure is plantwide. The teams have to cooperate to improve this measure. They can improve plantwide productivity by loaning team members to another team during times of decreased business in their area and by solving problems across team boundaries. Some organizations use a combination of facility-wide incentives (such as gain sharing) and team incentives to encourage cooperation across teams. In general, we recommend that teams have at least one measure that they share with other teams to keep them focused on the big picture.

- *The incentive system must be completely transparent to the team members.* People have to completely understand the system so they can calculate their own bonus correctly. In fact, it is best if they do their own calculations. After all, the purpose of the incentive system is to draw attention to the critical measures, and when team members make this calculation, what they typically focus on is not how much money they made but rather how much money they *could have made.* This is a powerful motivator, but it becomes lost in a system that is not transparent to team members.

- *Self-report measures such as surveys of teamwork, cooperation, and communication will be counterproductive if they affect the incentives.* These are often valid measures of team performance, but including them in the incentive calculation means that the measurement system will be paying the teams to cover up problems. The self-report measures can be used in the measurement and feedback systems but not in the incentive calculation.

- *The issue of raising standards to earn incentives in the future has to be addressed.* As mentioned earlier, these systems should last several years. Does the company want to pay the same money for the same level of performance as it did last year, or should the company raise the bar? These are not simple questions. Either choice sends a strong message and it's important that this message be consistent with other messages the company sends. Lincoln Electric, which serves as a model of pay-for-performance plans, does not raise the standards on which incentives are paid (Hodgetts, 1997). In our experience, the best solution may be to "raise the bar and sweeten the pot."

- *The company must decide how the incentive system will calculate performance scores that fall below expectations.* In the extreme case, if the team's score is below expectations, or negative, will the team members have to pay the company back? Not likely. In the more common case, the composite score is positive but some measures are below expectations, and the team thus has a negative score. For example, Table 9.1 presents one month's performance data for an assembly team. Note that the quality measure is below expectations

Table 9.1   Assembly Team Incentive Calculation

Assembly Team Performance	Data	Effectiveness	Goal	Incentive Points
Quality (35 percent) Defects per unit	.40	–17.5	.15	0
Productivity (10 percent) Book$ per labor hour	$300	5.00	$350	5.00
Cycle time (15 percent) Average cycle time in days	12.5	15.00	12.5	15.00
On-time delivery (24 percent) Percent jobs finished on schedule	89	7.50	95	7.50
Assembly start (15 percent) Percent jobs set up when scheduled	75	7.50	85	7.50
Group performance index		17.50		
Total incentive points				35

and hence has an effectiveness score of –17.5. Therefore, this measure is subtracting 17.5 points from the composite score. On the surface this seems fair, however, but it is important to compare it to the way management is compensated. In this company, managers receive no bonus when they fail to meet goals, but this failure does not take away from their bonus on other goals. In management's incentive system, this is the equivalent of turning any negative effectiveness score into a zero. In the interest of equity, the assembly team adds 17.5 to its composite score to remove the negative score, giving an incentive score of 35. This procedure sends a consistent message. It is interesting that this company raised the goals every year, so the teams had to improve to earn the same incentive as the year before. This raising of the bar is a part of the corporate culture and is also consistent with management's incentive plan.

Case Study: Plastics Manufacturing Team Incentives

Chapter Two presented the case study of the AT Plastics manufacturing team. This team is just beginning to use its incentive system. From the outset, they will have thorough knowledge of the measurement system through participating in its development and through using the system for six months. They will also have had two days of problem-solving training and six months of problem-solving experience with their system. For ready reference, here are the measures the team used:

1. Culture Survey (Employee Satisfaction and Communication)

2. Cleanliness Test: number of "B" size particles

3. Cleanliness Test: number of "C & D" size particles

4. Additive Test: Percent pass

5. Budgeted versus actual expenditures of fixed plus selected variable costs

6. Percent Yield (Prime product compared to total production)

7. Raw Material Inventory (compared to supply for thirty days of production)

8. Number of Lost Time Accidents

9. Number of Approved New Safety Procedures

10. Customer Satisfaction Rating: Overall score (a customer developed index that contains items for on-time delivery, quality, accuracy of packaging labels, and accuracy of invoices)

Of these ten measures, the first is a self-report measure. The next eight come from data developed in the course of operations, and the last tracks how well the team is doing with its customers.

The funding mechanism for the incentive comes from the plant's profit. That is, if the plant makes a profit then there is money for the incentive system. For purposes of this example, say that there is enough profit to allow $250 per team member in the incentive pool this quarter. Then each team member can now earn up to $250 each based on team performance. The team performance results for a given month might look like the ones in Table 9.2 (please note that this is not actual data).

For the incentive calculation, the self-report measures are dropped from the system, since keeping them in the system would tend to hide problems. The importance weight for the Culture dimension (5 percent) is simply added to the Percent Yield measure, bringing it to 15 percent. An incentive page is created in the spreadsheet to reflect this change. See Table 9.3.

Note that this team retains the negative effectiveness score for one of its quality measure in the composite score. Thus poor performance on this measure is costing the team 10 percent of the possible bonus. Unlike the assembly team in the example in Table 9.1, this team works in a company where poor performance in one area does adversely affect a manager's overall bonus. However, this company does not raise the goals every year, so if the team maintains this level of performance next year, it will receive the same bonus.

Table 9.2   Plastics Team Performance for a Month

Example Data	Data	Effectiveness
Culture (5 percent)		
Employee survey	5.00	5.00
Product quality (20 percent)		
Cleanliness test B (7 percent)	1.20	1.43
Cleanliness test C + D (7 percent)	0.22	5.51
Additive test (percent pass) (6 percent)	14.29 percent	−6.00
Cost control (10 percent)		
Actual to budget (per quarter)	10.00	10.00
Production (15 percent)		
Percent yield (10 percent)	92 percent	7.39
30 days' sales of raw materials (5 percent)	32.00	1.00
Safety (25 percent)		
Approved safety implementations (10 percent)	4.00	6.67
Lost time accidents (15 percent)	0	15.00
Customer satisfaction (25 percent)		
Customer survey	94 percent	7.00
Group performance index		53.00

Source: Adapted from AT Plastics, Inc. material. Used by permission.

To calculate how much they would earn, the team members take an average of their incentive composite scores for the three months of the quarter. Since this average composite is a percentage, they simply multiply the average by $250. For example, if their incentive composite averaged 40 for the quarter, the team members would each get 40 percent of $250, or $100, as seen in Table 9.4. What will probably happen is that they will become very concerned about the $150 they didn't earn.

One hundred dollars may not seem like much of a bonus, but it gets the team members' attention. The purpose of team incentives is not to rectify problems in the compensation system but to focus the team members on the key indicators of business success and

Table 9.3   Plastics Team Incentive Sheet

Example Data	Data	Effectiveness
Product quality (20 percent)		
Cleanliness test B (7 percent)	1.20	1.43
Cleanliness test C + D (7 percent)	0.22	5.51
Additive test (percent pass) (6 percent)	14.29 percent	−6.00
Cost control (10 percent)		
Actual to budget (per quarter)	10.00	10.00
Production (20 percent)		
Percent yield (15 percent)	92 percent	12.39
30 days' sales of raw materials	32.00	1.00
Safety (25 percent)		
Approved safety implementations (10 percent)	4.00	6.67
Lost time accidents (15 percent)	0	15.00
Customer satisfaction (25 percent)		
Customer survey	94 percent	7.00
Group performance index		53.00

Source: Adapted from AT Plastics, Inc. material. Used by permission.

Table 9.4   Plastics Team Incentive Calculation for a Quarter

Incentive Basis	Calculation
Plant profits this quarter:	$92,000
Minimum to fund incentives:	$60,000
Amount per employee in bonus pool per quarter:	$250
Average incentives index this quarter:	40 percent
Quarterly performance bonus:	$100

Source: AT Plastics, Inc. Used by permission.

create a business partnership. The incentive system accomplishes this. As a result, the team meetings become even more like business meetings.

Problems such as the additive test identified in the measurement system in Table 9.3 are diligently worked through the problem-solving process. The team follows up on the resulting action plans. From the team's perspective, it is their business and their money that's at stake.

This incentive system begins conservatively. Surveys from the Hay Company find that incentive pay typically ranges from 5 percent to 10 percent of an employee's base pay if the base pay rate is competitive (Gross, 1995, p. 148). The $100 in this case is less than 2 percent of base pay for these team members, but they could have made 4 percent. The company expects to enlarge the bonus pool, but it wants to proceed very carefully. The last thing the company wants to do is to back off the incentive system and demotivate the team members. By using the measurement system without incentives for six months, the company estimated the incentive payments for the remainder of the year to make sure the system was affordable. The company can also use these estimates to project the cost of the incentive system for the following year.

Slicing Up the Pie

Should all team members get the same amount of incentive? This creates a design conflict between a simple system where everyone gets the same amount and a more complex system where team members may get different amounts as a function of their base pay or their individual contribution. The company should make these decisions carefully, because there are two masters to serve: simplicity and equity. A system that is overly complex will hurt motivation because teams that cannot calculate their own bonus tend to lose interest. A system that is perceived as inequitable will create resentment among team members. Either situation will probably result in lower morale.

Basing Shares on Base Pay

Dividing up the team bonus as a function of base pay becomes an issue when there are substantial differences in base pay rates, as often happens in cross-functional teams. This issue becomes critical when people have pay at risk, since the at-risk amount is typically a percentage of the base pay. It is clearly appropriate to divide the team bonus according to base pay rates when team members have big differences in base pay *and* they have pay at risk. It is less clear what to do when there is no pay at risk. In this case, the teams themselves should have input in the decision. Teams may not want base pay to affect the size of each team member's bonus, because it adds more complexity to the calculations and reduces the sense that they are equal partners in their team's business.

Basing Shares on Individual Contributions

Team members often fail to contribute equally. This phenomenon, known as "social loafing," increases as team size increases. Many teams can deal with this problem through peer pressure and progressive discipline. However, some teams use incentive pay to address the problem. For incentive pay to work in this fashion, each team member has to be evaluated individually. Some teams use a team performance appraisal completed by the coach, or some form of 360-degree assessment, to determine each person's share of the team bonus. These procedures create their own set of problems as well as additional bureaucracy. Numerous companies have dismantled these systems as a result of the politics generated by the judgments required to determine the ratings.

For a monthly or even quarterly payout, judgment of individual contributions are usually too burdensome. These judgments are more often done on a yearly basis. Xerox takes a unique approach to annual raises, which connects individual contributions to the team's improvement efforts. As discussed in Chapter Five, each team member owns a measure or set of related measures of team performance. When the team begins an improvement effort on one of the measures, the "owner" enlists the help of other team members for certain tasks directed at that improvement effort. If team members fail to follow through on their agreed-upon tasks, they will be rated down when annual raises are determined. This way each person knows ahead of time what will happen. They also have a choice, reflected in their actions, of receiving an equal or less-than-equal annual raise. This is a worthwhile procedure because it revolves around the improvement efforts of the business and because people know what to expect ahead of time. As a result, there is a sense of fairness rather than a sense of playing politics.

Success and Failure in Perspective

If a team gets too caught up in its score, it loses sight of the purpose of the measurement system. The purpose is to stimulate feedback and problem solving rather than to make judgments about success or failure. In other words, it's about learning and continual improvement. If teams identify too much with their success, then they quit learning from their success. They also become afraid to take risks—because they might fail. However, if teams focus on learning, they are focusing on the process that will lead to success. In this regard, a lot can be learned from failure.

To learn from failure, however, a team has to focus on what it can change rather than on what it can't change. Think of it as focusing on possibilities rather than on why the failure is "not our fault." When faced with a failure, most people will try to blame something or someone outside of themselves. Alternatively, they may say, "It's hopeless. I shouldn't have tried in the first place." These tendencies usually increase when people are in a group. The "reasons" for the failure get reinforced. However, if a team focuses on possibilities, it may note the barriers to success and look for possible ways to deal with those barriers. The key is for team members to get into an observer and problem solver mode rather than a mode where an individual's self-worth has to be defended.

Protecting self-worth in the face of failure only leads to more failure or less risk taking.

Successful teams will experience empowerment and the accompanying responsibility for their slice of the business. As a result, they will ask for more resources. They may also ask for more decision-making authority. Since this kind of success is why organizations implement teams in the first place, it is important to be prepared to handle these requests, so teams will maintain their momentum.

A good measurement system provides very little opportunity for a team to fool itself. Low-performing teams become more noticeable, and their dysfunctional group dynamics tend to get worse. At the same time, research shows that team self-confidence consistently predicts team performance. (See, for example, Campion, Medsker, & Higgs, 1993; and Hyatt & Ruddy, 1997.) How does the measurement system affect a team's self-confidence, especially when that team is performing poorly? How does a leader build a team's self-confidence in this situation? These are critical questions that will almost certainly arise; no one wants to be caught by surprise on these issues.

There is also the problem of uneven performance across teams. A manager can easily have a strong team and a weak team next to each other. How should the manager treat the low-performing team? One approach is to focus the team on measures at which it is likely to succeed, thus building the members' confidence and willingness to take risks. Another approach is to tackle the problem head on, making expectations crystal clear. Resistant members of the team may need one-on-one meetings with follow-up. The manager will have to help team members become comfortable with taking the risks necessary to achieve high performance.

Summary

Since the purpose of teams is to turn employees into business partners, incentives add the finishing touch to that transformation. Incentives add power to a performance measurement system.

That's all the more reason to make sure that the measurement system contains the right measures and that teams are able to solve problems in their areas of the business. Most teams will jump at the chance to be business partners, when it is presented to them in the right way.

A team member was leading a team meeting. On the board he had written the following: "Not if but *when* the incentive system begins, how are we going to be ready"? This team's members wanted to make as much money from the incentive program as possible, so they were planning performance improvements they wanted to make. They identified problems based on their measurement system, determined causes, and developed action plans. They assigned responsibilities to themselves. They role-played a meeting in which they had to present their case to a group of engineers from whom they needed help solving a problem with engineering drawings. Their coach sat in the back of the room occasionally asking them questions to make sure they had considered the business issues sufficiently. He asked questions like "What are the engineers going to get out of this?" and "How will you show them that your idea will improve cycle time and reduce errors?" They eagerly answered these questions. This team was fired up about making improvements in "their business." What more could you ask?

Assessing Your Team

Think through answers to the following questions:

1. What are the pros and cons of using team incentives in your organization?

2. Design an incentive system that aligns with business strategy. How is it funded? How is it paid out? Who gets the incentive? When does it begin?

3. How are managers rewarded in your organization? To what extent are those rewards consistent with team rewards?

4. How will your incentive system handle business downturns?

5. How will your system handle changes in goals and capital investments that improve work processes?

6. How will your system handle part-time and temporary employees?

7. How will you be prepared for your incentive system to work? What if some teams greatly exceed their goals? What if these teams consistently earn more incentives than other teams? What if they ask for more resources? What if they ask for more decision-making authority?

8. How will you handle a low-performing team?

Menu of Sample Measures for Hard-to-Measure Teams

Accounting Measures

❑ Number of departmental errors (payables, receivables, posting, invoicing, cash deposits, payroll, costing, and so on) per employee

❑ Percent of reports redone

❑ Percent of on-time reports to management

❑ Percent of audit action items corrected within specified time period

❑ Timeliness of reports compared to department overtime expense

❑ Departmental costs per employee

Data Processing Measures

❑ Number of data entry or programming errors per employee

❑ Percent of reports issued on time

❑ Number of reports or copies of reports eliminated per employee

❑ Data processing costs as percent of sales

❑ Number of reruns

❑ Number of restarts

❑ Number of JCL errors

Note: This Appendix is reprinted from Joseph H. Boyett & Henry P. Conn, *Maximum Performance Management: How to Manage and Compensate People to Meet World Competition*, 1988, pp. 90–99. Copyright © 1995 Glenbridge Publishing Ltd. Used by permission.

- ❑ Total data processing cost per transaction
- ❑ Number of minutes of CPU downtime
- ❑ Percent of target dates met
- ❑ Number of incident reports (by hardware, software, or operators)
- ❑ Average response time to problem reports
- ❑ Percent of time on-line response time is greater than five seconds
- ❑ Number of data entry errors by type

Engineering Measures

- ❑ Percent of new or in-place equipment or tooling performing as designed
- ❑ Percent of machines or tooling capable of performing within established specifications
- ❑ Percent of operations with current detailed process or methods sheets
- ❑ Percent of work runs on specified tooling
- ❑ Number of bill-of-material errors per employee
- ❑ Percent of engineering change requests dispositioned in established time period
- ❑ Percent of engineering change orders per drawings issued
- ❑ Percent of material specification changes per specifications issued
- ❑ Percent of engineering change requests to drawings issued based on design or material changes due to drawing or spec errors
- ❑ Percent of documents (drawings, specs, process sheets, and so on) issued on time
- ❑ Number of line and supplier quality defects due to engineering errors

General Management Measures

❏ Number of grievances per hourly employee
❏ Percent of absenteeism
❏ Percent of hourly and salaried turnover
❏ Warranty costs/sales revenue
❏ Percent of product defects by product or department
❏ Percent of quality costs to operating costs
❏ Timeliness of shipments indexed to overtime expense
❏ Dollar cost of various expenses per employee
❏ Number of reports submitted per period

Human Resource or Personnel Measures

❏ Personnel costs per average number of employees
❏ Recruiting costs per number of recruits retained
❏ Training costs per average number of employees
❏ Cost of wage increases per average number of employees
❏ Cost of lost production due to labor problems per average number of employees
❏ Number of days lost production due to labor problems per number of days worked
❏ Number of days lost to absenteeism per number of days worked
❏ Number of employees who leave per average number of employees
❏ Number of employees with one year service per number of employees one year ago
❏ Number of employees with more than one year service per total number on employees
❏ Training costs/training days
❏ Training days/trainees
❏ Recruiting costs/recruits interviewed

- ❑ Recruits selected/recruits interviewed
- ❑ Recruits accepting/offers made
- ❑ Number of interviews per person hired
- ❑ Percent of new supervisors or managers completing basic supervision training within x days of promotion or appointment to position
- ❑ Dollars/hours outside training
- ❑ Percent of assessments of outside training submitted on time
- ❑ Percent of insurance claims processed on time
- ❑ Percent of attendance
- ❑ Percent of overtime hours
- ❑ Percent of turnover
- ❑ Percent of absenteeism
- ❑ Number of full time equivalent employees
- ❑ Number of recruits remaining on job after twelve months per number of recruits accepting employment
- ❑ Number of accidents
- ❑ Time lost due to accidents
- ❑ Ratio of supervisors or managers to workforce
- ❑ Benefit cost as percent of compensation
- ❑ Percent of implementation of performance appraisal recommendations
- ❑ Percent of accuracy of employee answers on company knowledge test
- ❑ Percent of sick leave utilization
- ❑ Percent of errors in processing personnel records
- ❑ Number of requests for transfer
- ❑ Dollar cost for testing applicants
- ❑ Percent of tardiness
- ❑ Ratio of employees available for promotion to total employees

❑ Percent of adherence to job classification or reclassification schedules

❑ Percent of new hires completing orientation within x days

❑ Percent of supervisors or managers who have completed basic supervisor training

❑ Number of department report or record errors generated per employee

❑ Number of investigated accidents

❑ Percent of hours lost due to investigated accidents

❑ Number of first aid cases

Marketing or Sales Measures

❑ Total dollar sales

❑ Ratio actual to projected sales

❑ Percent of new account sales

❑ Percent of new product sales

❑ Total number of new orders, accounts, new product orders

❑ Total number of accounts

❑ Dollar gross margin

❑ Dollar marketing or sales expense

❑ Total dollar sales/number of orders

❑ Total dollar sales/sales expense

❑ Sales expense as percent of dollar sales

❑ Number of sales per salesperson per day

❑ Total sales/number of calls

❑ Total sales/potential sales

❑ Total quotations (contracts presented)/total sales calls

❑ New account presentations/new account calls

❑ New product presentations/new product calls

❑ Sales expenses/total calls

❏ Profit as percent of total sales

❏ Number of pricing errors per time period

❏ Sales this year/base year sales

❏ Percent of previous year sales

❏ Sales growth in real (adjusted) terms

❏ Accounts receivable/average daily sales

❏ Selling hours/dollar sales

❏ Number units sold/weeks

❏ Number new customers gained

❏ Dollar revenues/dollar sales costs

❏ Dollar revenues/dollar sales quota

❏ Number prospects per week (month)

❏ Average quality rating of prospects

❏ Profit before tax (PBT)—year-to-date

❏ Capital returns—year-to-date

❏ Dollar return of capital—year-to-date

❏ Sample (demonstration) expense as a percent of sales

❏ Travel and entertainment as a percent of sales

❏ Dollar value or number of invoices past due

❏ Percent of accuracy sales forecast

❏ Percent of pricing variations to standard

❏ Orders incorrect per orders processed

❏ Customer complaints per period

Maintenance or Tool Room Measures

❏ Percent of machines or operations on preventive maintenance

❏ Percent or number of machine or operation breakdowns

❏ Percent of active machines or tools capable of holding design tolerances

❑ Percent of machine downtime due to maintenance

❑ Percent of tools or fixtures checked out before each release

❑ Percent of unscheduled overtime to total time

❑ Ratio of actual to planned equipment utilization (in hours)

❑ Percent of scheduled downtime

❑ Percent of unscheduled downtime

❑ Percent or hours of maintenance downtime

❑ Number, hours, or percent of machine stops due to operator errors

❑ Percent of downtime due to materials shortage

Material Control Measures

❑ Dollar inventory to dollar sales

❑ Percent of obsolete materials

❑ Percent of accurate inventory count per total cycle count

Production Department Measures

❑ Percent of on-time orders shipped to the next department

❑ Percent of lots or pieces accepted versus total lots or pieces

❑ Percent or dollars of scrapped or reworked output versus total output

❑ Percent of operators or assemblers checking their work to recognized plans or process instructions

❑ Number of machines or operations fully complemented with capable tools, gauges, process sheets, and documents, and properly lighted

❑ Percent of operators fully competent to perform assigned work

❑ Percent of unscheduled overtime to straight time

❑ Dollar rework or scrap per setup

❑ Number of grievances per employee or department

❑ Percent of reworks or rehandles (number of jobs)

❑ Percent of reworks or rehandles (hours)

❑ Number or percent of quality assurance defects (by type)

❑ Percent of seconds by type or cause

❑ Dollars, pounds, or percent of scrap by type or cause

❑ Dollars or amount of rework or scrap per setup or start-up

❑ Number of shipping errors by type or cause

❑ Number of bill-of-lading errors

❑ Dollars inventory spoilage

❑ Percent of defects or off-quality by type or cause

❑ Number or percent of errors or processing mistakes passed on to other departments

❑ Number of short lots

❑ Percent of lots or orders completed or shipped on time

❑ Frequency of production schedule adjustment

❑ Units or dollars of production behind schedule

❑ Average production time by type of product

❑ Percent of efficiency by department

❑ Percent of actual to standard production

❑ Number or percent of hours lost due to scheduling problems

❑ Percent of lots, orders, or jobs late due to plant errors

❑ Units, hours, or days of production backlog

❑ Ratio of setup or start-up time to available time

❑ Dollar expense or spending variance to budget

❑ Dollar direct labor cost variance to budget

❑ Total dollar cost variance to budget

❑ Dollar energy cost per unit of production

❑ Dollar total manufacturing cost per unit of production

❑ Dollar shipping costs

❑ Dollar value of surplus or obsolete inventory

❑ Dollars of actual versus estimated materials cost

❑ Dollar inventory shortage

❑ Actual versus planned inventory dollars

Production Control Measures

❑ Percent of stock-outs indexed to inventory dollars

❑ Percent of back orders

❑ Percent of in-house schedules missed

❑ Percent of machine downtime due to parts shortage

❑ Percent of late deliveries

❑ Work in process and finished goods inventory turns

❑ Percent of orders staged complete

Production Planning or Scheduling Measures

❑ Percent of deviation between actual and planned schedule

❑ Percent of on-time shipments

❑ Percent of utilization of manufacturing facilities

❑ Percent of manufacturing facilities at maximum utilization

❑ Percent of overtime attributed to production scheduling

❑ Percent earned on assets employed

❑ Ratio cost of consumable supplies to cost of production materials

❑ Ratio cost of parts and materials to production costs

❑ Percent of on-time submission master production plan

❑ Hours of time lost waiting on materials

❑ Number of days receipt of work orders prior to scheduled work

❑ Percent of turnover of parts and material (annualized)

❑ Percent of accuracy order status checks

❑ Percent reduction of cost of inventory from previous year

❑ Percent of on-time issuance of daily status report

❑ Number, pounds, or dollars of delayed orders

❑ Percent usage of internal sources for semi-finished materials or components

❑ Percent of back orders

Purchasing Measures

❑ Dollar purchases made

❑ Percent of purchases handled by purchasing department

❑ Dollar purchases by major type

❑ Percent of purchases per dollar sales volume

❑ Percent of "rush" purchases

❑ Percent of orders exception to lowest bid

❑ Percent of orders shipped "most economical"

❑ Percent of orders shipped "most expeditious"

❑ Percent of orders where transportation allowance verified

❑ Percent of orders with price variance from original requisition

❑ Percent of mail not metered

❑ Percent of "personal" mail

❑ Percent of orders "cash discount" or "early payment discount"

❑ Percent of major vendors—annual price comparison completed

❑ Percent of purchases—corporate guidelines met

❑ Elapsed time—purchase to delivery

❑ Percent of purchases under long-term or master contract

❑ Dollar adjustment obtained/dollar value "defective" or "reject"

❑ Purchasing costs/purchase dollars

❑ Purchasing costs/number purchases

❑ Dollar purchases/number purchases

❑ Dollar value rejects/dollar purchases

❑ Percent of shortages

❏ Dollar value orders overdue/average daily value purchases

❏ Dollar value orders outstanding/average daily value purchases

❏ Dollar inventory/dollar sales

❏ Average cost per requisition

❏ Average labor cost per requisition

❏ Average lead time for purchases

❏ Average time purchase request to issuance of purchase order

❏ Ratio number of requisitions received to number forecast

❏ Vendors or suppliers percent of on-time performance

❏ Vendors or suppliers quality rating

❏ Vendors or suppliers percent of standards conformance

❏ Stock-outs per time period indexed to inventory dollars

❏ Percent of purchase order changes

❏ Percent of purchase orders that require expediting

❏ Percent of late receipts versus total receipts

❏ Percent of purchases shipped other than the normal transportation method or lot size

❏ Percent of lots received with inaccurate piece count

❏ Number of departmental errors per employee

❏ Percent of orders received defect-free versus total orders received

❏ Percent of orders received late versus total orders received

❏ Percent of suppliers providing error-free parts

❏ Percent of suppliers who have formally committed to quality and productivity improvements

❏ Percent of approved or certified suppliers versus total suppliers

Research and Development Measures

❏ Actual costs/budget costs

❏ R&D costs/company profit contribution (actual or estimated)

❑ Number or dollar value of new products developed (last year, five years)

❑ Number or dollar value of process improvements (last year, five years)

❑ Number or percent of hours overtime

❑ Number or percent of hours on scheduled assignments

❑ R&D total cost as percent of gross (or net) sales

❑ Percent of cost reduction objectives met

❑ Percent of product development delivery (target) dates met

❑ Number years payout of research investment (actual or projected)

❑ Product development actual/planned costs

❑ R&D managers/R&D employees

❑ R&D technical personnel/R&D nontechnical personnel

❑ R&D postgraduate staff/R&D graduate (or nongraduate) staff

❑ R&D support staff/R&D technical staff

❑ Percent of turnover (technical personnel)

❑ Dollar value (actual or estimated) of new products or process improvements versus total R&D cost

❑ Percent of projects on schedule

❑ Percent of projects within budget

Secretarial and Clerical Measures

❑ Number of retyped letters or reports per employee

❑ Percent of absenteeism

❑ Percent of word processing pages retyped

❑ Percent of phone calls returned on time

Quality Control Measures

❑ Number of inspections, tests, or audits per employee

❑ Percent of product models or lots of products audited

❑ Percent of product models or lots tested before pack out

❑ Percent of reported problems corrected within specified period

❑ Percent or number of tests or inspections performed versus number specified in the standards

❑ Number of QC staff/total plant personnel

❑ Number or percent of product lots moved to next department or shipped with formal release by quality control

❑ Percent of gauges or other test equipment recalibrated on schedule

Receiving, Shipping, and Warehouse Measures

❑ Pounds or dollar value of orders damaged per employee

❑ Percent of receiving errors per documents processed

❑ Percent of material processed on time

❑ Percent of overtime per straight time

❑ Percent of orders processed on time

❑ Dollars shipped to the next station per employee

❑ Orders damaged per orders processed

❑ Percent of inventory accurate or in the proper location during cycle count

❑ Percent of orders rotated first in, first out

❑ Percent of inventory shrinkage to sales or total inventory

❑ Percent of orders shipped complete

❑ Pounds or dollar value of orders returned per total orders

❑ Percent of orders shipped on time

❑ Percent of orders shipped requiring adjustments

References

Alonso, M. (1999). A look inside BCBSSC Myrtle Beach Operations: Redefining the team implementation strategy. In S. D. Jones & M. Beyerlein (Eds.), *In action: Developing high-performance teams* (Vol. 2). Alexandria, VA: ASTD Press.

American Productivity Center (1986). *White collar productivity improvement: Results of the American Productivity Center's two-year Action Research Project.* Houston: Author. Available from American Productivity Center, 123 N. Post Oak Lane, Houston, TX 77024.

American Quality Foundation and Ernst & Young (1992). *Best practices report: An analysis of management practices that impact performance.* (Also called "The International Quality Study.") New York: Author.

Balcazar, F., Hopkins, B. L., & Suarez, Y. (1986). A critical, objective review of performance feedback. *Journal of Organizational Behavior Management, 7* (3/4), 65–89.

Boyett, J. H., & Conn, H. P. (1988a, Summer). Developing white-collar performance measures. *National Productivity Review,* 209–218.

Boyett, J. H., & Conn, H. P. (1988b). *Maximum performance management: How to manage and compensate people to meet world competition.* Macomb, IL: Glenbridge.

Campion, M. A., Medsker, G. J., & Higgs, A. C. (1993). Relations between work group characteristics and effectiveness: Implications for designing effective work groups. *Personnel Psychology, 46,* 823–850.

Deming, W. E. (1982). *Quality, productivity, and competitive position.* Cambridge, MA: Center for Advanced Engineering Study, Massachusetts Institute of Technology.

Deming, W. E. (1993). *The new economics for industry, government, education.* Cambridge, MA: Center for Advanced Engineering Study, Massachusetts Institute of Technology.

Felix, G. H., & Riggs, J. L. (1983). Productivity measurement by objectives. *National Productivity Review, 2* (4), 386–393.

Gilbert, T. F. (1978). *Human competence: Engineering worthy performance.* New York: McGraw-Hill.

Goldratt, E. M., & Cox, J. (1986). *The goal: A process of ongoing improvement* (Rev. ed.). Croton-on-Hudson, NY: North River Press.

Gross, S. E. (1995). *Compensation for teams.* New York: AMACOM.

Gross, S. E. (1997a, June). *Compensating and Rewarding Teams: How to Design and Implement Team-Based Reward Programs.* Workshop presented at the Best of Teams '97 Conference, Chicago, IL.

Gross, S. E. (1997b, January). When jobs become team roles, what do you pay for? *Compensation and Benefits Review,* 48–51.

Guzzo, R. A., Jette, R. D., & Katzell, R. A. (1985). The effects of psychologically based intervention programs on worker productivity: A meta-analysis. *Personnel Psychology, 38,* 275–291.

Hammer, M., & Champy, J. (1993). *Reengineering the corporation: A Manifesto for Business Revolution.* New York: HarperBusiness.

Heninger, C. (1994). *Performance by criteria matrix.* Corvallis, OR: Author. Craig Heninger may be reached by phone at (541) 758–5436.

Hodgetts, R. M. (1997, September). Discussing incentive compensation with Donald Hastings of Lincoln Electric. *Compensation and Benefits Review,* 60–66.

Hyatt, D. E., & Ruddy, T. M. (1997). An examination of the relationship between work group characteristics and performance: Once more into the breach. *Personnel Psychology, 50,* 553–585.

Jensen, B. (1997, March/April). Make it simple! How simplicity could become your ultimate strategy. *Strategy and Leadership,* 35–39.

Johnson, S. T. (1996, September). One firm's approach to team incentive pay. *Compensation and Benefits Review,* 47–50.

Jones, S. D., & Moffett, R. G. (1998). Measurement and feedback systems for teams. In E. Sundstrom (Ed.), *Supporting work team effectiveness.* San Francisco: Jossey-Bass.

Jones, S. D., Powell, R., & Roberts, S. (1990). Comprehensive measurement to improve assembly line work group effectiveness. *National Productivity Review, 10* (1), 45–55.

Jones, S. D., Buerkle, M., Hall, A., Rupp, L., & Matt, G. (1993). Work group performance measurement and feedback: An integrated comprehensive system for a manufacturing department. *Group and Organization Management, 18* (3), 269–291.

Kaplan, R. S., & Norton, D. P. (1992, January–February). "The balanced scorecard—Measures that drive performance," *Harvard Business Review,* pp. 71–79.

Latham, G. P., & Yukl, G. A. (1975). A review of research on the application of goal setting in organizations. *Academy of Management Journal,* 824–845.

Lawler, E. E. (1999). Creating effective pay systems for teams. In E. Sundstrom (Ed.), *Supporting work team effectiveness.* San Francisco: Jossey-Bass.

Lynch, R. F., & Werner, T. J. (1992). *Continuous improvement: Teams and tools.* Atlanta, GA: Qual Team.

Mohrman, S. A., Cohen, S. G., & Mohrman, A. M. (1995). *Designing team-based organizations: New forms for knowledge work*. San Francisco: Jossey-Bass.

Mohrman, S. A., Mohrman, M. M., & Cohen, S. G. (1994). Organizing knowledge work systems. In M. Beyerlein & D. Johnson (Eds.), *Advances in interdisciplinary studies of work teams: Vol. 2. Knowledge teams: The creative edge*. Greenwich, CT: JAI Press.

Phillips, J. J. (1991). *Handbook of training evaluation and measurement methods* (2nd ed.). Houston: Gulf.

Phillips, J. J. (1995). *Measuring the return on investment in training and development: Exhibits, exercises, and notes*. Birmingham, AL: Performance Resources Organization.

Pritchard, R. D. (1990). *Measuring and improving organizational productivity*. New York: Praeger.

Pritchard, R. D. (1995). *Productivity measurement and improvement: Organizational case studies*. New York: Praeger.

Pritchard, R. D., Jones, S. D., Roth, P. L., Stuebing, K. K., & Ekeberg, S. E. (1988). Effects of group feedback, goal setting, and incentives on organizational productivity [Monograph]. *Journal of Applied Psychology, 73* (2), 337–358.

Rummler, G. A., & Brache, A. P. (1995). *Improving performance: How to manage the white space on the organization chart* (2nd ed.). San Francisco: Jossey-Bass.

Schilling, D. (1998). Building a team measurement and feedback system to drive performance. In J. J. Phillips, S. D. Jones, & M. M. Beyerlein (Eds.), *Developing high-performance work teams*. Alexandria, VA: American Society for Training & Development.

Seaman, R. (1997, September). Rejuvenating an organization with team pay. *Compensation and Benefits Review*, 25–30.

Index

How to Use the CD-ROM

Press the little button and open the cupholder on your computer. Remove the saucer from the envelope on the facing page in this book. Put the saucer in the cupholder. Close the cupholder. (OK, it's a saucer holder.) Follow the directions in Chapter Seven for what else to do.

Teams on Track

Teams on Track is a program developed specifically to accompany the measurement approach described in this book. The software can be obtained at this Web site: http://www.mindspring.com/ ~teamperform/. Teams on Track provides step-by-step instructions for the user for activities at the end of Chapter One and Chapter Two, which develop the context for the measurement system. Teams on Track then has the team make decisions about measures that result in a completed version of the spreadsheet described in Chapter 7. For questions about Teams on Track, contact the Web site listed in this paragraph.